IN THE ARENA

IN THE ARENA

BATTLE-TESTED STRATEGIES
TO SECURE YOUR FUTURE

JULIE CALZA

LIONCREST
PUBLISHING

IN THE ARENA
Battle-Tested Strategies to Secure Your Future

ISBN 978-1-5445-3163-2 Hardcover
      978-1-5445-3162-5 Paperback
      978-1-5445-3161-8 Ebook
      978-1-5445-3951-5 Audiobook

To the kids we were, carrying the burdens we did,

thinking we knew it all while just trying to make it through.

To our son who brought the most unimaginable light

to us both and continues to impress us each day,

and of course to the ridiculous dog that reminds us not to

take life too seriously. There's always time for play.

CONTENTS

INTRODUCTION

THERE IS SOAKED. Then there is soaked to the bone.

From head to toe, camouflage paint covered my exposed skin, framed by the hard-worn cammies with all matter of mess covering it. One boot-covered foot was planted on the ground. The bright red dog tag intertwined in the boot laces glimmered. In the dark, swampy scene around me, I stared down at my other foot, naked and resting over my thigh. This pale, wrinkly foot had carried me through for weeks; a smile crossed my face, cracking mud on my cheek. I nearly laughed out loud knowing it had to carry me many more miles.

I sat with my stupid smile, stealing this moment for myself in the constant drizzle while trying to replace wet socks with dry ones in the hard five minutes we had before needing to move again. Once my foot-care micromission was complete, I resecured the pockets of my ILBE pack, then lightly kicked Kinley next to me. Like many of the men who didn't care about their feet in these moments, Kinley was fixated on eating. My nudge was to alert him that the signal to move was approaching. We would be heading to Camp.

There. The hand signal. Rifle at the ready, we stood carefully, one by one within our teams, and fell into squad column formation to continue through the dark, wet, overgrown tropical path.

As we came into view of the comical makeshift gate, I felt the eyes of the guard hidden within the trees land upon my back. Deep breath. Calm. Security. As Marines, we are never really alone, but only another of my kin in arms could properly understand that feeling, that next-level herd mentality. As we passed through the Camp kill zone, then through the makeshift bottleneck into Camp, we were quickly directed to debrief.

The building was called the theater, but from the outside, it looked as if the engineers had taken many liberties in putting it together, and calling it a theater was more of a joke than anything else. Just before we made it to the door, an officer stepped out. His uniform looked brand new, and so did he. He quickly caught sight of us, shuffled out of the way, and held the door.

The amount of gear we each had forced us to sit with empty seats between us. No one had broken the silence, and no one was eager to. We were ragged but stone-faced. No one was willing to give a clean onlooker any glimpse of the cards we were holding, the thoughts dancing through our heads.

The young officer let the door shut and walked to the front of the room to join another just like him who had yet to make eye contact with any of us. They looked at each other, maybe not having decided who would start, or maybe having the wherewithal to question the tactics to follow even momentarily. Regardless of what the look was for, one fired up the little projector and illuminated on the wall a PowerPoint slide of learning objectives. At the top were the words "Improvised Explosive Device (IED)." This initial slide, bullet by bullet, broke down for us what we would take from this training. Their voices shook as they reviewed the material. Because they were new training instructors, we struggled to take them seriously, but we kept quiet and let them work through their slideshow, showing us how we could be killed.

To this day, I remember this moment and the sequence that followed. I don't remember it for its horrifying content. I don't remember it for the people in that room who later died because of IEDs. I don't even remember it because of how ridiculous it was to learn about IEDs via a slideshow. I remember it because someone who had never walked in our shoes was telling us how not to die. This was the first time I'd realized how ironic this situation was, even though it wasn't the first time it had happened.

Multiple slides contained images of toppled Humvees; some even boasted the newer MRAPs and how they fared in comparison when faced with IEDs. The images graduated to those of bodies torn apart with pieces of uniform still attached, lone boots still containing feet, women and children lying dead after having been blown into a ditch alongside a dirt road.

The images didn't startle me. They didn't horrify me. They didn't even cause my heart rate to change. None of us stiffened, we were relaxed in our seats, and Kinley, very obvious to us, slept with his eyes open. I struggled not to fall asleep.

In contrast, the officers grimaced with each click of the computer, their body language unsure and uncomfortable. About halfway through the presentation, one of them stepped out, as if it was too much for him to bear. Throughout the presentation, the tempo of their voices changed; their tones would break before fully pulling themselves back together or trading off who was speaking.

When I realized just how desensitized we were and how tolerant we were of being briefed on how not to die this way, I realized they were not teaching us to thrive through these challenges but instead how to survive long enough to complete our mission.

The most ineffective component of this ironic training session was the source. We knew they were new to the job: their uniforms lacked decoration, and their rank displayed just how fresh they were, although if it hadn't, their demeanors would have given them away anyway. They had never experienced what we had, much less the tactics they were trying to teach us. Their brass revealed that they'd completed a college degree and had received theoretical training about leadership and how to train others. Yet here they were teaching us how not to die when they had no experience in theater.

No military aims to teach us how to thrive, nor is it their responsibility to set us up for life outside the force. The problem is that our expectations have been so muddled through the time we spend being trained, talked at, and conditioned that we lose sight of the gap between service and self. That gap closes and we become our service, but if we don't take responsibility for ourselves and responsibility for the future of the family we accumulate along the way, then what is left when the service is done?

In the civilian world, uniforms don't give people guidance to question who is providing advice or telling you what to do. There are no ribbon decks donned on chests to signify our experiences. There are no ranks that clue you in on authority. People can call themselves experts despite never having done what they are claiming to teach. Age is a very misleading indicator yet really the only obvious one that exists in the civilian world.

You are responsible for making your own way. You can serve your country proudly while preparing for the life you will live postmilitary.

If you wait for the military to tell you what steps to take or to give you a PowerPoint briefing on how to be successful outside of the entity, you'll find yourself waiting forever. Then, once you have finished your time, what will you have left?

If you rely blindly on guidance without any responsibility for your part in getting where you want to go, how can you ever hope to succeed?

It's easy for those within the military or for other onlookers in your life to try to call your shots because those spectators aren't down in the arena with you. They are what they've been conditioned to believe and, whether they are in the service or not, are awaiting their next set of orders from whoever shows up to divvy them out.

This book aims to show you, to spark in you, the drive to find answers to what comes next. I've bound these words together so you can hack these answers from the get-go or build on the experience you have from a deeper level.

Thinking outside of your conditioning is a fight; it is not an easy path and is like stepping into an arena. Whether you are battling the nature you were born into or the conditioning you took on along the way, the biggest mistake you can make is not taking the first steps into exploring what would be possible if you tapped the opportunity around you.

Your biggest success comes long before you get where you want to go. It comes by putting boots on the ground and trying. You will take some hits and deal some misses. But you have plenty of shots left to take, and you will land them when it counts most.

There might be a mistake along the way, but in this arena you are fighting for your life...the one you have left to live.

Get into it, mud-caked boots and all.

How this battle goes relies solely on you.

STAGING AREA

I have heard the question: "How do you stay disciplined?"

The answer is: it's a choice everyone has.

But the choice becomes much easier when you take the time to determine what success looks like to you and why you want the life that success will bring.

Now close your eyes and visualize that success. Imagine what it would feel like living your life as if you have accomplished what you deem successful. Imagine what it would feel like to match your current pay grade with income from investments and not have to work each day, enabling you to focus on your passions. Visualize that life.

If you do not get a surge of excitement from your image of success, then maybe you're using a definition of success that you have been conditioned to see instead of what might bring you fulfillment. I cannot tell you what your image should be, and it won't work if someone else tries to motivate you to accomplish your goals. You have to see your goals, the ones you set, so you have the motivation to go toward them.

Brute force of blindly "doing" will not get you there. The excitement of elevating yourself above what you may feel is possible, then taking action to make progress toward that goal, is what will get you there.

Your personalized vision will enable you to take the necessary steps. And with each small step, making the choices each day to keep going becomes easier.

1. Figure out what you want to do (or be).
2. Determine why you want to do it (or be it).

Regardless of your goal, I'll show you how to take small steps to make big progress, how to go from not knowing who you are outside of your current role to how to secure your life separately from it.

This is not just about trading one never-ending cycle for another. It's about writing a life that excites you in real time versus settling for less in the hopes that one day your life will be different.

You don't have to be reliant on the military forever.

I served in the Marine Corps, and my husband is in the Air Force. I created my vision of success, then I reached it faster than I ever thought possible. I built a business doing something I am passionate about: helping military members and their families learn how to leverage their VA Loan benefit into profitable real estate investments and educating my community on how important it is to work toward financial freedom. I have had the honor of impacting thousands of lives along the way.

I know the challenges this community faces—I have been there myself—and I know how to help military members secure their postmilitary future.

Now I'm sharing that knowledge with you.

What are you waiting for?

It's time to get started taking steps to realize great success by your own definition.

CHAPTER 1

HACK IT

HOW MUCH TIME DO YOU SPEND thinking about what you want your life to look like one year down the road? How about five years? Ten years?

The average person overestimates what they can accomplish in a year and grossly underestimates what they can accomplish in a decade. This has always been a problem, but in our culture today, the "now" mentality is severely limiting a person's capacity to see themself across time. Most do not look beyond the year they are in, severely blocking themselves off from opportunity. So if you haven't devoted time to envisioning in detail what you want from your future, you are not alone. But taking steps to overcome these self-imposed limitations will free you to make serious progress toward goals that may feel overwhelming.

If I go to Target without a shopping list, I'm likely to get distracted. I'm likely to spend time wandering the aisles, looking around, and very likely to fill my cart with things that I didn't actually intend to get. Eventually I will decide it's time to go and head to the checkout line. When my total comes up, I might be surprised, but I will dutifully hand over my card to complete the transaction then head home. When I get home, I may even realize I forgot to get what I went to the store for in the first place.

If I go to Target with a specific list, a set of predetermined items I want or need, then I am on a mission. Yes, I may still get distracted and stroll, but my priority becomes getting those things into the cart and getting them home. When I get to the checkout stand, I pay the price, complete my goal, and feel like I accomplished something. Even if it's fleeting, there is satisfaction in it.

How can you hope to get what you want into your cart if you do not take time to determine what it is?

A gap exists between who you are now and who you want to be. The more distracted you get in the present moment, the wider the gap becomes. It widens even further when you realize there is a difference between what sounds good in the moment and what would bring you long-term fulfillment, the difference between what everyone says you should want and what you actually want from your life.

I would argue that gap is even deeper for military members and their families because they have the somewhat unique distinction of being issued a vision for their future. Everything about the military is designed to motivate you through achieving the next award, getting the next assignment for career progression, and attaining the next rank.

It is designed to motivate you to give the most possible, without showing you how each of those things really impacts your life. Awards and career diversity are meant to lead to getting to the higher rank more quickly. A high rank means being responsible for more people, which translates into more hours devoted to the job, at a pay rate that is not weighted to that responsibility. Having the larger patch on the uniform feels good; the ego really likes the authority.

But if you've been issued this goal based on the agenda of others, how can you expect fulfillment to come from achieving it? If you are only focused on making the next rank, what steps could you possibly be taking to secure your own vision of your future?

Trust me; where you are right now is connecting you to somewhere amazing in the future. The clearer a picture you can develop of what you want, the more likely you are to get to the checkout stand with your deepest desires in your cart. Once there, the price you pay is in the actions you took to get there, and developing the vision is that crucial first action.

So I ask you again, how much time do you spend thinking about what you want your life to look like one year down the road? How about five years? Ten years?

How clear can you get on those visions?

QUESTIONING "IF"

When I get my gears turning about what I may want from my life, I quickly find *What if I can't do it?* floating through my mind. It's clear many people have this same struggle of wondering if they have the right formula to accomplish their wildest dreams. What's interesting is how some who encounter this question of "if" hesitate to even try to reach for their goals. It's so easy to get wrapped up in whether we can hack it that we are utterly robbed of progress we could be making toward that very dream.

So instead of asking yourself, "What if I can't do it?" ask yourself, "What if I do it?"

What if you get everything you ever wanted?

What if you're able to identify all that you've yearned for—then you get it?

What if it really was as simple as going to Target, putting things in your cart, and then going to the checkout stand?

The payment due would be the actions you took to get there. Have you attempted to pay the price? Have you taken any action? Or have you neglected to develop your vision because you have convinced yourself it's useless to try?

Beautiful things start to happen when you not only have a vision of what you want but also start opening yourself up to what it would feel like if you had it. So not only does a vision help you feel good; a vision also gives you a destination. But you can never get there if you don't give yourself the opportunity to get started heading in that direction.

I saw a TED Talk where Patti Dobrowolski talked about how important it was to physically draw your future. Take marker to paper and illustrate what you see in your head. She claimed it didn't matter if you were a terrible artist and you drew stick figures, that the most important thing was making the physical connection between the image in your head and putting it to paper.

I'm not talking about material possessions here. Those might be pieces of the puzzle of your future, but usually those possessions you want are arrows serving as symbols of your desires. Do you want the newest gaming console because it helps you escape the day-to-day existence that you are unhappy with or because growing up, you could never have things like that, and it makes you feel good being able to buy them now? Those options are not the exclusive reasons you may want it, but you can see how the material desire can point to a deeper thought pattern.

You may draw a big house with your happy family out front and that car you always thought was cool parked in the driveway. The house is shelter and safety; no, you may not "need" a big one, but that symbolizes financial comfort. The car serves the same purpose. I point this out because when I drew my picture, I felt silly and a little guilty. I knew I didn't need everything in it in order to be happy, but then I realized the point is to draw a dream. Aside from the laws of physics and humanity, the point is not to be "realistic." The point is to challenge your own definition of what is possible. If you're going to dream, don't limit yourself by fear of *What if it doesn't happen?* Dream big, my friend.

After discovering Dobrowolski's TED Talk, I spent the next three years of my life with a little hand-drawn picture I had made. My picture seemed audacious when I drew it, but it became a background staple that was just there on my desk. I saw it every day. What's funny about it though is that I didn't even realize the moment it came true. I just kind of looked at the picture one day and realized I had everything I had drawn. I thought it would take ten years or more, and I admit that when I drew it, a part of me felt like it would never happen. But I had replaced that with a focus on what it would feel like if it did.

It's easy to renegotiate with yourself when you encounter obstacles, and we are quick to sacrifice our deepest desires for short-term relief now. If I hadn't had the picture for reference, I could have easily changed the end goal. I could have easily veered off course or just changed the vision over and over and then felt like I wasn't making progress, not realizing it was because I kept moving the target.

Without the end goal—the picture—you don't really know where you're going. With it, you can take the end goal and map out a route to get there. You can set markers for yourself along the way.

It's what marathon and distance runners do; they count light posts or landmarks. This not only shows them how far they've come but also how much further they have left to go.

You can do the same.

Set yourself markers; some will be bigger than others.

Some will be like the checkpoints in racing video games, the ones that give you a special ability or power boost of speed. Others will just be the little turns along the way and not as eventful. But it is still progressing; it is still miles down.

For example, if your picture is your happy family in front of a dream home, with a dream car in the driveway, and you with a dream job, there is a way to make those goals into tangible, bite-sized steps. To get the dream home and car along with less stress, which will help with happiness, you'll need stable finances.

Your first power boost benchmark is to pay off consumer debt.

Your light posts to stay on track and see your progress to get to this point would be as follows:

» First, set aside a savings of $1,500 so you can confidently STOP using the debt. If you already have this amount in savings, your goal should shift toward tackling the debt versus building the savings, then come back to the savings after the debt is cleared.

» Organize consumer debts (everything except car payments and mortgage) in order from smallest to largest.

» Concentrate any extra funds monthly toward the balance of the smallest debt first, making minimum payments on everything else.

» Pay off each of your debts in order from smallest to largest.

This is how you build goals effectively. You not only have to determine where you are going, but you need to set yourself checkpoints along the way to stay on track. This will not only help you get there, but it will also keep you motivated along the way and help you see how far you've come. The progress you have made. (We will go more in depth with specific benchmarks and how to plan your route, along with plenty of examples, in later chapters.)

Understand, your biggest dreams are attainable as long as you define them and interrupt any voices (in your head or otherwise) that try to focus on them not happening.

One day you'll wake up in that picture. You will have worked for it. You will have put in the time, the energy, and the effort for it, and it'll be here.

But if you don't spend any time thinking about what you want that picture to look like, it's never going to arrive. If you don't spend any effort mapping out how you're going to get there, you won't ever head toward it. If you let yourself be slowed down by questioning whether it can happen, what can you ever actually accomplish?

When you are tempted to doubt, to stray into worrying, you're wasting your time. Interrupt that toxicity by asking yourself, *What if it did happen?* What if you got that picture exactly as it is drawn? Let yourself have that hope, have that motivation. What do you have to lose? The world is dark enough as it is. Be your own guiding light.

It is not a matter of what if you fall...but a matter of what it would feel like if you flew.

DONE IS BETTER THAN PERFECT

People fall. Just because you get tripped up along the way does not mean you have failed. We can't talk about setting big goals, making progress, and having these amazing visions without discussing what to do when you trip. We can't discover the possibilities of being able to fill the cart, clear the payment, and walk out of the store without talking about the fact that at some point, you will stumble. You will make a wrong turn, you might pick up the wrong thing, or you might go down the wrong aisles, so it may take more time to get what you're looking for.

If you go into this process thinking it will be perfect, then you're setting yourself up to fail. It's the same as if you only ever think about the possibility of failing and don't take any action. We must acknowledge that the process of moving toward your picture won't be perfect, while protecting ourselves and our own mentality from dwelling on what it would feel like if it wasn't perfect.

It will be challenging to see your progress along the way. Especially when you expand a vision out across years or along a lifetime. But that's where your benchmarks are going to save you. You don't have to look at this big, intimidating thing all the time; you just have to look at the next marker. Or maybe a little past that one to the next big power boost in order to stay excited.

Paying off one credit card may only feel exciting for a day or two, but it's still getting out from under that debt and real progress toward breaking out of a cycle that 80 percent of Americans find themselves trapped in.

It is human nature, especially in a Twitter universe, to want instant gratification. People want answers in 280 characters or less. They want to live their lives 280 characters at a time. But you're writing a novel here. How exciting that novel is, how joyful it is, and how it feels to read relies solely on you. So you can go for 280 characters at a time, but if you are not being intentional about connecting those points toward a goal, man, that would make for a pretty choppy story.

You can go for buying those things that you don't have the money for, racking up the debt because it will momentarily feel good to drive that car, to have that new motorcycle.

But ultimately, what do those things help you accomplish other than feeling good for just a bit? What story of your life are you telling with those choices?

I have heard it said a lot, and I'm sure you have too, that money cannot buy happiness. I'm not here to argue that point because I see all too often that people bank on it.

They bank on making that next rank and then expand their expenses quickly to fill the financial space it gets them.

But I will add that what money and financial stability can do is bring us security. In the world today, that security can bring flexibility and freedom that the generations before us did not have access to.

So understand the societal tendency to pull toward instant gratification. Because when you understand that impulsivity, you're able to catch yourself. If you can strengthen that self-control, you will already be leaps and bounds ahead of the majority around you. You will be giving yourself the gift of space to refocus on that picture you drew, to recenter on the path you're on, and to recalibrate for your next benchmark.

When you stumble, and I say "when" because you will, all is not lost. It can be recovered with those steps of recalibrating.

Let's say you're aiming toward that benchmark of paying off debt, but then you use a credit card again or something unexpected happens. To get motivated to get back on track using this framework, all you need to do is calibrate and refocus on the end goal. See, once you have your vision and take time to think about the route, it becomes easier to ground yourself and always have a way back when you get off track. You are also less likely to get off track when you actually know the track.

Small steps make big progress. Some days it will feel like two steps forward and one step back. Other days it will feel like you have made huge jumps forward.

Regardless of what day you are in today, enjoy the journey and revel in what it would feel like if you got everything in your picture.

QUICK TIPS

» To pay off consumer debt, you must stop using it. Otherwise, you're just trapped in a never-ending cycle, being manipulated by a system designed to imprison you.

» Take time to think about what you really want your life to look like one year from now, five years from now, ten years from now. Physically draw a picture. This does not mean you should just draw material things; draw yourself happy and use symbols for things that aren't material.

» Draw that picture and start now. Seriously, no matter how small you think the steps are, get started making progress toward that vision.

If you don't think about what you want to do, why you want to do it, and see yourself doing that thing and understanding how it will feel, the world will pull you away. You will be pulled into other people's agendas, other people's urgencies, and other people's priorities. Very quickly you will be led into living an unintentional, reactive life.

Simply going with the flow.

I have a hard time believing you want your life to resemble that of a dead fish in a river.

CHAPTER 2

ONE PERCENT

"WE HAVE ALWAYS RENTED. We weren't in a place to be able to buy. We don't know if we can now, but we see how much we are spending each year to rent and would rather put that toward something we own."

This was the answer Kristen Kern gave to the question I ask any buyer: "What made you decide to look into buying a home?" It wasn't a groundbreaking answer. In fact, it was well enough like nearly every answer I hear. In our initial conversation, nothing in particular made the Kerns stand out as different. They came from a background typical of a young military couple. They didn't have resources available to them that were above and beyond the norm.

What they would go on to accomplish wouldn't happen because they had some secret sauce you don't have access to. Well, maybe that's not entirely accurate; you could call it secret sauce if you are so inclined. If you are, then let's say the secret sauce is that they were open-minded. They were coachable, willing to learn, and willing to make a clear effort to define a long-term goal. Because of this secret sauce, we were able to develop a plan for them to secure their first home, a first investment for them to live in and begin to grow a future of their dreams. I helped them develop a clear picture of what they wanted to accomplish across the next five years, then we set up benchmarks for them to work on along the way to stay on track.

Matt Brink's answer wasn't much different than the Kerns'. "We want to put our housing allowance to something. Like we want to try to make something from it; we want a house that's ours. Plus, what we pay in rent for the apartment is the same as what a house would be."

He sat across the conference room table holding Sarah's hand as she smiled. They looked at each other, clearly dreaming of what the future would hold. We went on to talk about what they'd love to have in their first home together. They asked a lot of questions, I answered, and we set up a plan custom to their goals. Nothing completely out of the ordinary, no significant content standing out as different from the Kerns' consultation that had happened that same year.

The two couples wanted different things specific to the home itself and were open to different areas, but both were realistic sets of criteria, and they'd be purchasing within the same budget range, which was also realistic to their individualized criteria.

MOVING FORWARD

The Kerns loved talking about the next steps. As we toured homes, they loved hearing about what aspects of the individual homes made them ideal for either future rental possibilities or future resale. Their favorite questions to ask were about cost-efficient improvements that could be made to each home and what benefit that could lead to in the investment itself. Anytime they were tempted to veer from the budget, I reiterated how important staying within it was, not just for this home but also for their future vision.

The Brinks, unlike the Kerns, really wanted to focus on this first home before getting too far into the future with planning. Anytime I brought up resale and rental possibilities, they redirected to discussing what upgrades they wanted to make in the home and how they'd definitely need to paint the cabinets if this one was going to work. They wanted to stretch their budget to get something new, not unusual. I encouraged them to stick to the budget they were most comfortable with, but of course it was their decision to make. They weren't ready to think further in advance than the one goal in front of them at this moment, which was buying a place of their own.

EXPLORING OPTIONS

After plenty of searching and evaluation the Brinks selected a beautiful new home to be built. The floor plan was perfect for their needs, and the options they were able to select made their eyes light up. They were excited and I was happy for them, not just because they were getting something they really loved but because they'd heeded my advice and were within their personal budget, not the max the lender had qualified them for (those two numbers are rarely the same for home buyers).

The build was quoted at six to eight months for completion. I told them based on my experience, I would recommend planning for nine months and then being happily surprised if it was finished sooner. I also reassured them we would be able to track progress and that the timeline would be fine-tuned the further the build came along.

They paid a $1,000 earnest deposit to secure the contract, which was set to be applied toward their own closing costs at the end of the process. They would not need any additional out-of-pocket money to buy the house. A down payment was not required because they'd be using the VA Loan, and in the contract, we'd gotten the builder to cover their remaining closing costs and even provide incentive toward a good chunk of their upgrade options. A great deal—I was thrilled for them.

Meanwhile, the Kerns were still exploring their options. I could visibly tell Kristen and Nate enjoyed the journey of seeing the homes, but they had the good sense to pounce when they found something they liked. Even at this time in the marketplace, it was competitive enough that they hadn't secured the first two homes we had offered on. It's not just about getting the home; it's about getting the right terms too.

UNDER CONTRACT

When the Kern family went under contract, it wasn't an air of nervous excitement. It wasn't jumping and cheering. It was a calm, business-like review. We reviewed the next steps extensively, and I answered all of their questions. This is nothing unusual. Most home buyers either feel this trepidation right off the bat, or they get really excited and then they pause, and reassurance comes a little later. The Brinks were the latter, really excited off the bat, then once the excitement settled, we were able to review next steps more in depth.

Kristen and Nate Kern had a longer than normal close of escrow at the same time that Matt and Sarah Brink were waiting on their home to be built. Both had a comparable mix of nervousness and concern along the way. The Kerns had a clear vision of what they wanted, and this first home was a big benchmark along the way. Knowing this gave them drive and comfort. They made a calculated decision.

The Brinks made an equally calculated decision when choosing to buy a home and when selecting their home. The Brinks were jumping for joy when they went under contract; they couldn't have been more excited and described it as their "dream home" multiple times. They felt confident and assured, though a bit nervous about the time frame.

Home prices began to climb quickly. People at work told Matt Brink he was crazy to buy a house because he would only be living there a few years anyway. A couple of Sarah's friends who lived on base told her they'd never consider buying while stationed at Luke Air Force Base because pricing was "so high." And Matt's parents, who had foreclosed on a home they were upside down on from buying in 2005, told him the market would crash again and he would be screwed.

The Brinks' contract price was locked in, so their home would be worth more at closing than what they were paying. Even though they were so excited and confident, these outside voices took their toll. Ultimately, the Brinks decided to cancel the contract to buy their first home.

When the Brinks called me to let me know they wanted to cancel, I reviewed market data with them and encouraged them to look at the first home as a tool. All the same information I had given the Kerns. I would never pressure someone into buying a house though; my aim and my business's aim is always to educate. So Matt and Sarah did not close on their new build.

Instead, they moved from their rental off base into on-base housing.

TWO YEARS LATER

Two years after getting the keys to their very first home, Kristen and Nate Kern were ready for their next power boost, their next big benchmark. They were nearly debt free and had been saving to have some cushion going into the next home. Their five-year vision was to be debt free and to own three homes. Their ten-year vision was that income from rental properties was set up to match Nate's income from active-duty military service.

The plan I had outlined for them would have them moving into the next home as a primary residence so they could use the VA Loan again, which would prevent them from having to do a big down payment. They would be renting out the home they had lived in the last two years.

Going into this next purchase, based on our plan, the Kerns knew this next home would be their home for longer than two years, so they were more particular about what they wanted. We found the perfect fit, and within four months of starting the search again, they got the keys to their second home.

At the same time, the Brinks decided to reapproach the home-buying process. In the past two years, they had spent roughly $64,800 in BAH (Basic Allowance for Housing) to on-base housing, yet the new build they had been set to purchase and ultimately canceled would have secured them a monthly payment below that amount, which would have included room for utilities within their BAH. And the home they had been under contract to purchase had significantly increased in value, by approximately $86,480.

Despite having thrown $64,800 to base housing and losing out on $86,480 in home equity that would be theirs had they bought the house, the Brinks still harbored a lot of hesitation as they began their search again. Their expectation was to get a similar home at a similar price to what they had secured before canceling. However, they were considerably more limited since pricing in the area had gone up. It was a great learning experience about the importance of getting into the first home.

Having that first investment gets you into the market, which provides more leverage and resources. The Brinks struggled to find anything they liked. They encountered a lot of obstacles mentally and were not willing to see the limitations they had placed on themselves as a result of taking advice from so many who had not accomplished what they were wanting to accomplish.

They were also still only focused on the short term, the next step, these 280 characters in a Twitter culture. I did my best to coach and advise them, to be supportive of their short-term goal while trying to help them see a longer-term perspective. Ultimately, they decided to put the search "on hold for a year to see what the market was going to do."

EXECUTING A PLAN

With a clear vision made, a plan to execute followed. Like clock-work, Kristen Kern messaged me to say, "We are ready." It was eleven months, nearly to the day, since they'd gotten keys to their second home and moved into it, renting out their first. The goal was to be in the market for the third home one year after the close of the second. Of course, we'd stayed connected throughout the time frame since I had first met them, so I wasn't surprised by the message. But given all I see in people losing steam and strug-gling to have the courage to get started, I'm always ecstatic to see them on track. We began work, having more logistics to accom-plish this time. They needed to do a refinance on the first home to free up the funds they'd need for the down payment to buy a straight investment. (Meaning to buy a home with the intention of immediately renting it out).

The refinance took roughly thirty days. Once finished, they were out looking at homes with a CalzaCo expert agent. Shortly after they had boots on the ground for this search, the world paused. The COVID-19 pandemic raged through, bringing state after state to shut down. The uncertainty throughout the market-place was palpable. It seemed like no one really knew what was going to happen, at least at first.

In times like this, the best thing to do is lean on data. Emotions are a survival mechanism deep within us, meant to trigger us into reaction. In modern society, it is so easy to be triggered like this and to get wound up in emotion, leading to impulsive decision-making that is not reliant on any real logical information.

Kristen and Nate asked me what to do. "We trust you; we will do what you tell us to do," they said. "So, what do you think?"

Trust is not something I take lightly. I built a business to protect military members, to guide military families, and to pour back into the military community. Yes, CalzaCo serves all sorts of people, but all of that service is for the purpose of being able to provide more resources for military members and their families. Anyone that trusts me or my team does so confidently; it's an honor and a deep responsibility.

The news being so fresh, my response was that we should give it two weeks. The shutdown was supposed to be only two weeks, but I suspected it would be longer. But I also suspected it would create an unbelievable opportunity. So many people would be waiting to see what happened, but once it was over, they would all flood back. There were just too few houses and too many people who needed shelter. "Give me two weeks to watch the data," I told them. "If it stays shut down, we need to jump in."

The world stayed paused. A supercompetitive market became a frightened and more balanced one. The Kerns found a great home and went under contract. I went under contract on an investment property too.

I advised all our clients to jump and said that it would be much harder once this time passed. There was opportunity, especially for military members buying with the VA Loan. Some listened; others didn't.

I reached out to the Brinks because it was the one-year anniversary of pausing their home search.

They said, "Obviously, now isn't the time. The market is going to crash."

MOVING ON

The Kerns got the keys to their third home three years and a few months after buying their very first home. They were debt free because they'd used some of the money from refinancing the first home to clear up what debt they had left. They kept ample equity in the first home so that all of their numbers still worked. They were following the plan. They kept a clear view of the vision throughout their time, and they got to their five-year goal with over a year and a half to spare. So they made a new vision.

At the time of this writing, it has been five years and six months since I first met Kristen and Nate Kern. They now own four properties and are in the market for their fifth. Nate recently sewed on Tech Sergeant in the Air Force, they have two kids, and Kristen works flexibly from home. They are debt free and rent from the rental investments they already own will beat Nate's Tech Sergeant pay once the mortgages of those homes are paid off. The tenants are paying off those mortgages for them, and as it stands, they profit enough from the rentals to have a very comfortable savings cushion which enables them to take a few vacations a year to make memories with their family.

If the Kerns sold all four of their homes now, they would make approximately $455,000 after paying off the mortgages. Even if the market were to dip, they would have ample room to hold on to their investments or to sell them without any losses because they stayed on track with their vision and made intentional decisions.

The Brinks did not buy a home. They are still living on base.

Today, the home Matt and Sarah were under contract for is worth approximately $199,360 more than the price they were contracted to purchase it. Since deciding to cancel the contract on their home purchase, the Brinks have spent approximately $151,800 for on-base housing, based on the Basic Allowance for Housing (BAH) in Matt's pay and the fact that Matt has made rank, further increasing his BAH. So if they had purchased a home, it would have increased in value substantially, and they would have been making those payments against the balance.

WHAT DID NOT WORK FOR THE BRINKS

The Math

The Brinks weren't willing to consider the math, how much they would pay monthly for something they could own versus renting on-base housing. As I stated earlier, the home that the Brinks were originally under contract to purchase is worth $199,360 more than their contract price. In addition, the Brinks would have made payments toward their balance. The lower balance owed combined with the increase in value would have led to more money in the Brinks' pocket if they sold the home. Meaning they would have gotten a massive return on the money they would be paying for housing versus with renting (even on base). Once rent money is spent, it's gone.

Even if the home had not gone up in value, the Brinks would have had a fixed payment on the home, one that they were comfortable with at the time of purchase. So as BAH went up and as Matt made rank and their income went up, their costs would have stayed the same. They still would have been building equity by paying down the loan balance on the home while also creating more flexibility in their budget as time passed.

If the home value somehow went down, it wouldn't change the fact that their costs would have stayed the same, providing them with consistency and elbow room as their income grew. Not to mention, they would still have an asset that they could leverage.

The Brinks blocked themselves from so much opportunity by being shortsighted on what homeownership would have empowered them to accomplish.

Moving the Target

Somewhere along the way, the Brinks shifted from buying a home to put their BAH to good use, to buying a home to make money, to not buying a home at all. They changed the end goal; they moved their own target so much that they ended up not hitting anything at all.

No wonder they were overwhelmed!

Going through the home-buying process with a goal of trying to make money leaves you exposed to making long-term decisions based on short-term situations. Meaning you only see things that could prevent you from making money versus the stability that owning a home provides. The return on investment you get each day is a secure shelter for you and your family at a cost that works for your budget. No landlord to sell the home unexpectedly, leaving you scrambling, or raising the rent to an amount you cannot afford. No changing standards, meaning your dog can no longer live at your home without fear of consequence. As your income or housing allowance goes up, your mortgage payment doesn't automatically rise with it.

Over time, a home is not just a way to potentially make money. It's a vehicle of stability, helping to better sustain you as you work toward financial freedom.

Losing Sight of the Goal

The Brinks stumbled by allowing others to cloud their vision of owning a home as security. They went into the process with good intentions of having a home of their own and wanting to put their BAH to good use. Along the way, they let a lot of voices in that didn't live in their shoes. They also did not want to look further down the road past buying this first home. Owning multiple homes is not the path for everyone, but everyone does need a future vision of themselves in order to make intentional (and confident) decisions.

Matt and Sarah got so caught up questioning "what if" something went wrong that they became overwhelmed. Once overwhelmed, it was impossible for them to see clearly or even envision the amazing opportunities before them.

If the Brinks had been willing to take time to develop a vision of their future, a clear picture for themselves, it does not mean they would have been immune to people clouding their judgment or that it would have protected them from questioning themselves. It means that they would have had an image to ground themselves in. Instead of only having a slew of answers without knowing the questions, they would have had the guiding light of asking themselves, "Will this action help us achieve our vision? Will this step move us closer to our destination?"

But the Brinks didn't fail. In fact, this is an invaluable opportunity to learn. Matt and Sarah can choose to focus on what they didn't do, they can choose to avoid the topic because they feel shame, or they can look forward. They can develop a clear vision and set up benchmarks to aim for as they build to that bigger vision. They wouldn't be starting over because they have learned so much already.

WHAT WORKED FOR THE KERNS

Being Open-Minded

The Kern's were open to learning about what they could do; they were willing to take time to think about what they wanted the future to look like. Once Kristen and Nate discovered their vision, they were unwilling to risk sacrificing it. We built out the benchmarks, they were careful in making decisions, and yes, they were hesitant and scared along the way. But they let that end goal propel them. They were clear on developing criteria for homes because they were always asking, "How will this action help us achieve our vision?" They were not predisposed to being highly decisive people at all, and there was plenty of back-and-forth. But the clarity they'd developed helped them be decisive when they most needed to.

Leveraging Small Steps

The market changed a lot over the five-year time frame in which the Kerns were working toward their goal. But because of the care they took in developing their route, the market conditions had little impact on them making progress. They leveraged small steps over time. That first two years in their first home, they got comfortable. It wasn't perfect; they got out of some debt just to go back into other debt. They were unsure if moving again was really worth it. They were comfortable and could have stayed put. Yes, that house was still a great investment, and they would still be in a great place if they had stayed there. But because they grabbed ahold of that first opportunity, many more opportunities became available to them, opportunities they took because they wanted to achieve their vision.

Getting Started

Kristen and Nate took action to create one opportunity for themselves, which unlocked so many doors for them. Opportunity compounds over time. You do need to get clarity, then wait to have the courage to get started in order to take advantage of it. Do not be intimidated by how long it might take you to do something or get to a certain point in your life. The time will pass anyway. Isn't it better to spend that time making progress toward a future you really want?

SMALL STEPS MAKE BIG PROGRESS

Standing in front, looking at a five-year time frame, it seems like a really long time. But looking back on the last five years, it feels like it went by really quick. Isn't that a funny phenomenon? So how can we look forward at the next five years with that same perspective of time?

The crucial element is endurance. When I look back across the last five years of time, I remember hard times, of course, but they don't seem as hard as they did in real time. That's because while I was in them, they were taking a lot of energy, a lot of headspace. And when something is hard, it seems to drag out time. Whereas, when I am looking back at those times after getting through them, I am in a different headspace. I have greater perspective.

If we break a big goal that seems impossible into small steps, it's more likely we are able to complete them. If someone wants to lose sixty pounds, they're more likely to stick to it and get it done if they aim for two pounds at a time. This is where endurance comes in. Pacing yourself gives you a higher likelihood of making it to the finish line. Before you know it, you've dropped that weight. It was hard along the way, but when you get to that goal, you look back and it was worth it. Once you achieve the end result, the discomfort of getting there feels irrelevant, doesn't it?

If you spend the next five years taking steps to achieve a clear vision that excites you, achieving those steps along the way, no matter how small they may seem, will sustain you. Don't just focus on the next thing in life. Instead, focus on the next right step to get the greater thing you really want. Those are two very different things. That next right step you made over and over becomes miles of progress.

You've seen two couples beginning their journey from a remarkably similar starting point and continuing across the same time span. Kristen and Nate Kern kept a sustainable pace. Yes, they accomplished big things, but all the little steps they took along the way are what got them there. Matt and Sarah Brink have taken a lot of action, but it wasn't intentional and did not end up leading them to a much different place than where they started.

If that next step you take is a benchmark toward a greater vision, that's one thing. But if it's just the next thing in a string of random next things, is it really progress?

Aim for that big, audacious goal. But across time, plan for 1 percent progress each day. Prepare to buy the first house, then buy the first house. Once you do so, you have it in your tool belt to leverage toward making more progress.

QUICK TIPS

» Taking action on one opportunity will get you more opportunities. Get clarity on what you want, then take action!

» Not all benefits and returns are in money. All too often, I see people mistake a comfortable pattern for safety and security. But safety and security come from building flexibility for yourself. You need to be intentional about building flexibility in order to secure a future you want.

» Making a bad call does not mean you will have a bad life. We are all learning as we go. All the preparedness in the world will not prevent you from making a mistake. Look at everything as a learning opportunity, and don't let the possibility of a mistake stop you from taking action.

It's hard to be in the top 1 percent, but it is not as intimidating to look at incrementally improving 1 percent at a time.

Saving $10,000 is an intimidating goal for many people.

But it's easier to make 1 percent progress each day.

If you want to have $10,000, set aside $28 per day and you'll get there before a year.

Reading twenty pages per day leads to reading thirty books per year.

Saving $10 per day equals a savings of $3,650 per year.

Running a mile each day equals moving your body 365 miles per year.

Becoming 1 percent better each day compounds out to 37 percent better each year.

Progress doesn't have to be complicated; it just has to be intentional.

If the vision is the castle, small steps are the keys to get in.

CHAPTER 3

BRICK WALLS

"HOW DO YOU DO IT?"

That's the question I am asked most often at industry events, award ceremonies, by my own team members, and even by our clients.

They want to know how I've built my business so quickly, how it keeps growing, and how I do everything I need to accomplish both professionally and personally.

I have this funny answer I usually give: "I got really good at running really fast at brick walls. When I crash, I get up, take two steps to the left, and run at the next one." We chuckle and the conversation progresses to other areas.

They want the easy answer, the formula, but what worked precisely for one won't work for all. Resilience is the way, the commonality for anyone trying to get to a big vision.

My success didn't result from becoming good at running really fast at brick walls or obstacles; it is the result of taking the necessary steps to build resilience along the way so that when I encountered the brick walls, I could get back up, pivot, and keep going. I admit, my childhood experiences and Marine Corps training gave me an advantage when it came to resilience in building a business. However, anyone can learn the resilience needed to achieve their big dreams through exposure and embracing obstacles head-on.

Instead of viewing the brick wall in front of you as something you will crash into, that will hurt you, view it simply as an experience that you will learn from before moving past.

CRASH TEST

Alex seemed nervous as I asked him to give me a tour of the home he had bought a couple years prior. "Kinda weird," he remarked. "Last time you were the one showing me around."

I laughed and joked, "You're right, but you got this!"

As we walked through the home, he pointed out things that were on his list to fix and some changes they had made since moving in.

The tour ended in the master bedroom, and he stood in the doorway not really knowing what to do or say. I politely suggested we sit back at the dining table to review. He seemed relieved by the guidance, and we headed back down the stairs. Sitting at the table, Alex was fidgeting. I could tell there was something coming that he did not want to reveal. He had worked hard to qualify to buy this home; it was touch and go as he had begun the process. When he decided to look into buying, he had recently gotten stationed at Luke Air Force Base, Phoenix, which happened to be where he was originally from. So, he moved in with his mom temporarily when he and his wife separated. However, he soon discovered how much she was struggling to take care of herself, that the rental was in poor shape, and the landlord was increasing the rent. Because his mom was on a fixed income, she just couldn't make ends meet.

When I started to work with Alex, he had some credit recovery to do. He faced that obstacle, adjusted course, and was able to get around it. He didn't freeze. Instead, he put in consistent effort. It took some time, but he got it done!

We found a great home for him that was well within his budget. When he got the keys, he and his mom moved in. Although I tried to stay in touch, I had not really heard back from him since I thanked him for leaving CalzaCo a great review.

Just a couple months before the two-year anniversary of Alex closing on his first home, he reached out to me. He had become interested in selling his current home and buying another one. We set up a time to meet, and I was looking forward to helping him map out this next part of his journey.

We sat at the worn table, Alex was jumpy, and I was concerned. I went through the normal questions we like to start with to gather as much information as possible in order to build out a custom plan. Incrementally, the source of Alex's nervousness was revealed. The HOA had put a lien against the house, not because he had refused to pay but because billing got mixed up and he was too far behind to catch up by the time he realized it. As a result, it became a debt he couldn't get ahead of. He had bought a new sports car, and the $600 monthly car payment was also a strain. These additional expenses caused Alex to begin falling back to credit cards to fill the gaps, and he was in over his head.

With each detail he shared, it became more difficult for him to make eye contact with me. Yet with each detail he shared, I could also feel some of his tension release. Like saying it out loud was letting go of some hold it had on him.

I stayed silent but maintained warmth in my expression as he spoke, and I took notes along the way. When he was finished, he sighed, looked at me, and said, "I know... I really messed this up. I didn't listen, and I was just so stupid." He quickly looked back down, folding his fingers over and over in his lap.

Alex had called me because he wanted to move into a home better suited for his aging mother. He told me about his issues because he was concerned about the obstacles those would create in buying the next home. I wanted him to be able to keep the first home as an investment as he moved into the next, but this wouldn't be possible given Alex's situation.

This is why getting clarity on your vision is so important. Owning multiple properties is not the right route for everyone right off the bat. Real estate is a sound investment and an incredible building block for wealth. I would also argue it is the easiest pathway for military members to set themselves up for an abundant and stable life outside of the military. But it is not a one-size-fits-all solution.

Alex's five-year vision was to be able to take care of his mother and for her to have a better life, for him to be able to provide a stable place for them to live, and for his sister to be able to move in with them, since she was struggling too. Alex is in his early twenties, and at this time, he intends to spend a full twenty years in and retire from the Air Force. He feels like he messed up, not for himself but because he lost sight of how much it mattered to him to provide for his family. In addition, Alex didn't grow up learning anything about managing money or planning for the future. Of course it would be challenging for him to make long-term financial decisions.

Sitting next to him, I realized that Alex's biggest fear wasn't the weight of these debts or even qualifying for another home.

It was that he had failed and would not be able to move forward the way he could have if he hadn't made those fumbles.

I looked at Alex folding his fingers over and over, smiled, and said, "All of this is fixable. It'll be just fine. These are just steps, and you have plenty of options, as we discussed, to climb up them."

He looked surprised and replied, "You make it sound easy."

"Easy to assess, not easy to do," I pointed out. "But you've dealt with more difficult things than this. You've deployed and you've dealt with harsh work environments, plus, you've taken steps to set yourself up outside of work. You have a huge advantage that can help you with this."

"Yeah, you!" Alex quickly responded. "Thank you so much!"

I laughed and said, "No. Your house. You worked for this, and it's on your side to help you now. Yes, I was there to help and am here now, but you have accomplished big things before. Do not discount yourself."

Together we outlined the obstacles Alex needed to face to move forward, and I helped him see a few different routes he could take to address them. The initial investment he had made into his future by buying his current home gave him options. He could either keep it as a stable cost for housing as he worked through the other obstacles, or he could sell it and use the proceeds to get around these brick walls.

Ultimately, Alex decided it was best to sell and leverage the equity toward getting around these brick walls and getting into a home better suited to his family's needs. This also kept him on track with his vision of supporting them.

After some searching, and trying for a few homes that didn't work out, Alex found a home perfect for their needs. He was able to use the proceeds from selling his home to pay off all his credit card debt and the HOA lien and to invest in a down payment on the new home, while making sure his monthly payment was still within his budget. He could have paid down the car too, but Alex decided he didn't need the car. After closing on the new home, Alex traded the car for something better on gas and with a much better payment. After making those changes, he still had a bit in savings to help prevent him from being tempted into falling back on the credit cards.

He got a fresh start, but he didn't have to start over. When Alex worked hard to buy his first home, he was in similar debt. It took a lot of time and effort to slowly chip that away and get into a position to buy. Alex started building his own brick wall when he fell back into old habits. He knew what he was doing, but he became so fixated on the problem that he developed tunnel vision, which led to feeding the problem and creating a bigger one. He wasn't able to see solutions until someone pointed them out. Because of the progress he had made before buying that first home, not only did Alex have the first home to use as a tool, but he also had the resilience of having faced obstacles before. Additionally, he knew what it felt like to make big progress. That feeling you get when you achieve those benchmarks can become addictive if you let it.

Once you have a brick wall in front of you, whether you had a hand in building it or not, it is really hard to see the other side, much less any way around it. There is a reason why debt is frequently referred to as a hole—it's hard to get out of.

But you have to realize your tendency to fixate on problems and see how that blocks you from ever finding solutions before you can begin to reset your focus to that feeling that will motivate you.

If you get tunnel vision and only focus on what's right in front of you, then why not aim to control what's right in front of you? Focus on what it would feel like to overcome the obstacle versus focusing on the problem itself.

KNOW WHEN TO PIVOT

When I met with Alex, he knew he had to do something before things got worse, but he had no idea where to start. Alex felt like he had ruined the progress he had worked hard to make; he felt like he had failed. But the failure comes in not getting back up when you run into a wall. Just like opportunities compound, resilience does too. The more often you get back up, the easier it gets to get back up each time, so you are able to rebound more quickly and get back on course. The biggest mistake you could make is failing to learn along the way.

There is no sense in fearing problems that could arise. In fact, plan on encountering difficulty without knowing what it will be. Just know that it will come. Obstacles are opportunities to build resilience, and they are part of the journey.

Alex could not qualify to buy another house in order to continue forward toward his goal without addressing the debts he had accumulated. He wanted to live a debt-free life, and his longer-term vision was to be able to comfortably retire from the military. But brick walls were erected between him and his benchmarks. Alex could have easily given up and continued relying on habits he knew were not serving him. They had a home to live in, and it would have been comfortable for him to stay put and not strive to break out of the cycle he had become trapped within again.

But because Alex had the experience of breaking through this brick wall before, he recognized what was happening and decided to take steps to work around it.

If you don't have experience in breaking through, which helps you recognize the moments to pivot, don't worry. You will still know you've gotten to that crossroads.

If you are at a point where you are not moving toward a picture of what you want your life to look like, it's time to pivot.

If you are at a point where you are making progress toward a vision you really want to be living, but you find yourself unable to take another step forward on the path you are on, it's time to pivot.

When you inevitably encounter these difficulties, they will stop you. That's how you will know it is time to make a change. Something will prevent you from moving forward toward your vision. These moments are times to adjust, to reset. They are not signs to quit trying.

If you were watching a movie of your life, and you saw the main character stop digging literally just a couple feet shy of striking gold, would you yell at the screen? Imagine that character just stops and says, "Ugh, I'm tired of this," then walks away, back to where they were before they started trying. The movie gets boring as you watch them going through their day-to-day motions: drinking, eating, playing video games, maybe going on a trip. But you, the viewer, know they were RIGHT THERE. They were so close to getting everything they ever dreamed of. So freaking close to living in a vision they had thought was impossible. The movie ends, and yes, the story had some fun, and there was plenty to be grateful for along the way, but would you leave the theater frustrated that they had gotten that close and just quit?

We are the main characters in our own stories, so we don't get to see beyond what's in front of us unless we take time to envision it, then go after it. The journey will not be without dips and turns. But the process contains fun and plenty to be grateful for along the way. You get to learn from every peak and valley. And if you're able to fall in love with the journey, you're more likely to stay on course. Although there is nothing telling you not to appreciate where you are, do not use that as the excuse to remain stagnant instead of continuing forward. Keep building; keep moving.

Each obstacle provides an opportunity to pivot as long as you look around and make a decision.

Plan on falling, and plan on coming up on the brick walls. It's impossible to see what they will be; they are well camouflaged. But on the other side of each are more options and opportunities.

Imagine three doors in front of you. One won't work out, but if you do not commit to making the choice of trying a door, you lose out on all three. If you commit to a door and the decision you make is wrong, then make the next choice.

For example, another option that was available to Alex would have been to sell the vehicle and get something cheaper, and then use the extra savings to start tackling the credit card debt, smallest to largest. As long as he paid the HOA on time moving forward, the lien would stay as it was and be alleviated when he did sell in the future. As long as it didn't continue delinquency, it wouldn't add up to a bigger problem. Once the other debts were tackled, he could work on the lien too.

Once Alex got past those obstacles, he could qualify to buy the next home and potentially keep the current one as a rental property. If he got into that process and then decided it just wasn't working for his needs, he could then make a different choice.

I bet you have met people trapped in front of a brick wall who simply settle in and accept it as insurmountable. Or maybe you have been one of those people setting up camp, accepting the obstacle as the end of trying. Some who are stuck here become the quickest to criticize those that keep trying to move forward. Those that are stuck and cynical are the most dangerous to encounter because they thrive on getting others to join them.

When you run up on a brick wall, do not get frozen and stubbornly refuse to make another move.

Time will continue to pass. Do you want it to pass you by, or do you want to be in motion with it?

QUICK TIPS

» Stay pointed toward your end goal, even if you pivot. The route will not likely be a straight line, but if you constantly change your destination, you'll never make it to what you really want. The end game is not changing, but how you get there will not always go how you originally planned.

» See obstacles as opportunities to grow or to build strength in overcoming. What seems impossible to you now will one day be something that you can do with ease. Once that occurs, you may not even remember it as having been really hard.

» Use tunnel vision as an advantage. If you tend to only see what's right in front of you, then be intentional about what you allow right in front of you.

"I don't want to have to start over." That's a really common reason people use to justify not moving forward, but consider this: are you ever really starting over if after something doesn't work out, you get to start from a place of knowing that way didn't work? It might not be the progress you want, but learning the wrong way teaches you that the way you took wasn't the right way, so you can move on to another option. With each brick wall you encounter, you are gaining more experience. You are never starting over.

Get clear on what you want, aim to make steady progress, and give yourself the grace of knowing that when you get knocked off track, you can pivot and find your way back. When you encounter those obstacles, do not change the destination. Just plot a different course. It's scary to change course when you can't see how it will turn out, but fear is a part of being human.

CHAPTER 4

KNUCKLE-DRAGGER

GROWING UP, I SPENT SUMMERS with my dad in the Texas Hill Country. We always had to be on the lookout for deer when driving. Let me tell you, the saying "deer in headlights" is quite literally founded. The moment the deer's eyes caught the headlights, it would freeze in place, wherever it was. Not only would the deer not get out of the way of a moving car or motorcycle, but it would have a delayed reaction that caused it to leap in front of a vehicle at the last moment. So a driver unfamiliar with the deer's freak tendency may have thought the deer on the side of the road wasn't a threat, until the deer ran out and caused a severe accident.

It was impossible to know when the deer would react or how. They were unpredictable, erratic, and incredibly dangerous.

There is an instinct in all of us that is more similar to the deer than we may care to admit. It's left over from our days as Neanderthals having to assess any input for potential threats at any given time. A significant portion of our brains still reacts and behaves as if we are back in the caves listening for saber-toothed tigers.

If you're reading this, you more than likely do not have to face life-threatening situations anytime you are hungry, tired, or moving from point A to point B. But our brains so easily shift into a freeze, flight, or fight panic when we encounter conditions outside of our comfort zone.

So, any perceived oncoming pain or discomfort can trigger the "deer in headlights" response in humans.

Many times, we read this reaction as a sign that we shouldn't work through that challenge, when in reality, it's just a side effect of our evolution. That voice in your head, that knuckle-dragging Neanderthal, is a biological response that is meant to help you survive.

Survive. Not thrive.

GETTING UNCOMFORTABLE

Anytime you consider doing something different, your brain looks for reasons not to try it because it defaults to anything unknown as being unsafe. In addition to mental anxiety, you might have a physical response. Your body tenses up, it feels like you're holding a bowling ball between your shoulders, and your stomach feels nauseous. Each of these symptoms results from the voice in your head warning you that this unknown path is dangerous. This warning signal is ingrained in our DNA.

In the beginning of humankind, these instincts were crucial to survival. If a stranger approached your camp, these warning signals sounded because you didn't know the stranger's intentions, whether they wanted to become friends, collaborate on a hunt—or kill you.

It's natural to dodge "threats," yet many people are not aware of how far they go to avoid discomfort. In today's world, these deep survival instincts can easily cripple you from making progress toward your goals because any obstacle can trigger that freeze, flight, or fight instinct.

Freeze

When you're serving in the military, your basic needs (food, drink, and shelter) are met, and a pathway is laid out for you that gives you a framework for every step to come. Everything is so structured yet somehow manages to feel both rushed and delayed at the same time. "Hurry up and wait" is a common sentiment felt throughout the ranks.

It becomes incredibly easy to go stagnant, whether you are willing to admit it or not.

You're doing the same set of things day in and day out, waiting for the opportunity to promote, waiting for PCS orders, waiting for anything that could break it up. Even if you enjoy the work that you are doing, it is easy to get comfortable in it and get caught up in waiting for the next thing. This dangerous place is where dreams float away and are replaced by ambitions for things that might be possible but were never really what you were intentionally after. Soon your vision becomes buried beneath layers of outside influence telling you where you should want to go. Soon you may find yourself depressed and anxious but not having a clear reason as to why you feel locked in a dungeon.

This may not be as dramatic as a deer locked in headlights, but this withdrawal from intentional living is a version of freezing. You are still stuck like the deer in the headlights.

When that happens, ask yourself, "What am I afraid of?"

More than likely, you are unaware of the fears that are keeping you stationary. Without understanding what those fears are, it is impossible to determine if the knuckle-dragger in you is trying to keep you safe from a saber-toothed tiger and is therefore holding you back from your vision in today's modern world.

Getting stagnant is a version of shutting down; it is inactive avoidance. We recognize shutting down more readily when we are approaching something we do not want to confront or when someone tells us something we do not want to hear. And that part of us that aims toward our vision becomes buried and shut down waiting for the "right" time.

No one can issue you a perfect framework for your life without being familiar with your vision for it, so why wait for them to tell you how to get what you really want?

Your job is not catering to who you will become or want to become; no one is sitting back crafting the path for you to get precisely where you want to go. Your work is designed to accomplish the goals of the organization you work for (whether it's government based or not). The organization benefits when you get comfortable, while developing skills that may help the organization reach its goals faster. Plus, the more comfortable you become, the more likely you are to stay, even as you develop those skills. The organizations we work for rely on us to stay within a designated role, a box of limited thinking. Isn't it funny that we rely on them to give us the resources we need to live the life we want?

I am not saying quit your job. I am saying that your most important job is to put effort into breaking out of your comfortable patterns in order to develop yourself and make progress toward your own vision. Use your day-to-day work to gain leverage in making progress toward that vision. Be willing to be uncomfortable, because if breaking these patterns were easy, there would not be entire entities devoted to keeping people within them.

Fight

Fighting is not just getting into the ring and throwing punches or having a confrontation with someone. Many times, I see people fighting something without even realizing that's what they are doing.

For example, my clients Amy and Martin Thatcher purchased a home with much trepidation. They had dreams of becoming landlords and building a real estate portfolio, but they were paranoid about each step of the process, not asking questions for the purpose of receiving answers but asking questions then questioning the motivation of the answer, assuming others were looking to take advantage of them. They were never confrontational but were very aggressive and unwilling to take advice.

Not only did the Thatchers extensively question the motives of everyone involved in the process, but they also made decisions that were very different than what was recommended. It seemed like the decisions were different just for the sake of not wanting to take recommendations. I did everything I could to guide them and reassure them that every decision was theirs to make and if they were uncomfortable, they could cancel the purchase. They ended up closing on the home but not getting as much as I know they could have in the process.

A year later, the Thatchers reached out to me wanting to sell because the house was worth so much more than they had paid for it. I encouraged them to stay in the property because pricing had gone up so much and renting would be more than their mortgage payment, plus they were building equity in the home. However, they were convinced the market would crash at any moment.

I did my best to educate them about the market and made sure they understood they would likely need to pay capital gains tax[1] on the amount they made from the sale since they had only lived in the home a year and did not plan on buying another. I explained to them that due to capital gains tax, the market would have to go down over 15 percent for them to not make more than if they waited an additional year to sell their home. They wanted to move forward, and I agreed to help them sell.

As we went through the home-selling process, they were offended by the offers they received even though the offers were over asking price. Later the Thatchers were offended by the buyer's repair requests even though the Thatchers had been very thorough in their demands when they had purchased the home.

Because the Thatchers were unwilling to work through this process, a collaborative process they had never done before that would enable them to obtain the best outcome, the prospective buyer canceled the sale, and the Thatchers' home went back to market. This was okay because we handled it well and got new offers quickly, soon going under contract for the same terms. However, the Thatchers dug their heels in over and over again throughout the process. Fortunately, they were able to close.

---

[1] We will talk more about capital gains taxes in a future chapter.

When it came time to file their taxes for the year they sold their home, Amy reached out to me because they were upset about capital gains tax. I had prepared them for this reality, but she was just having a hard time facing it and wanted to know if I had heard of any new ways to get out of paying it. I sent her a resource and reference for a good accountant. She said that in hindsight, they wondered if they had made the right choice by selling. I reassured Amy that only they knew what was right for their family and that if they made the choice to sell, it was because it was the right one at the time, which made Amy feel better.

The Thatchers spent a lot of their time projecting their insecurities and fears onto others, unaware that doing so was holding them back from seeing the big picture clearly. They were so microfocused on every little interaction, trying to catch anyone that might be trying to pull something over on them, that they completely buried their own vision; they lost sight of their own goals. Their fight consumed them.

Fight is not the most common reaction I see from people. The most common is trying to escape it entirely.

Flight

I do not want to face that, so I will do this other thing instead.

Sound familiar?

Flight is an avoidance tactic.

The first benchmark in the process of buying a home is to get prequalified. It is totally normal for lenders to need supporting documents in order to finalize your qualification and give you the most accurate picture of what to expect in a monthly payment based on your purchase price options. It is not uncommon for good loan officers to recommend you do a few things in order to be able to get the best terms. This could be something like paying off a $300 credit card balance or finding an error on your credit report and helping you get it removed. The suggestions are unique to each borrower, so it's impossible to know what those suggestions would be for you until you provide the lender with the information they need and they review it properly.

Frequently, when a buyer gets with a lender to go through this process, they procrastinate when it comes to turning in documents or providing the lender with additional information. They avoid calls from the lender too. This is so common that we prepare our clients for what the process is like and what to expect, and we reassure them that it doesn't mean they cannot fulfill their goal of buying a house. In fact, this part of the process serves to make sure they buy within their budget and meet their goal in the best way possible. However, despite preparing our clients, this avoidance still happens frequently.

We can tell it is avoidance and this flight response because the client will continue to communicate with us, but they'll say things like, "Oh it's just been a busy week. I'll get that done today." Then they don't, even though they wanted to be moved into a home as soon as possible. Or they'll say, "Yeah, I'm just one of those people that need to be reminded. I definitely want to get that taken care of."

Of course we never pressure people, but many times, through reassuring them and asking more questions, we learn that they're worried they won't be able to qualify for as much as they need in order to buy what they want.

If you fear failure, your tendency will be to make choices in an attempt to avoid the pain you perceive that comes with failure. These choices will result in the opposite of your intention. They will put you in a position to fail.

Challenges of any level can trigger wanting to escape from them. The obvious problem with attempting to avoid failure is that it's rare for something to be handed to you without challenges along the way. And you are guaranteed to fail if you never try to move toward the goal.

Human nature is to escape pain as quickly as possible; it's a survival instinct embedded in our DNA to preserve life. If it's freezing outside, your cold fingers remind you to put on gloves. If your blood sugar drops, your body sends signals to alert you to eat so you don't pass out. If you exercise hard, your body needs more oxygen, so you get a sensation of feeling short of breath.

All of those signals serve you well, but you cannot thrive if you are allowing survival instincts to drive your life. This hypervigilance is exhausting. Constantly assessing for life-and-death threats uses too many inner resources, leaving little room to think about anything else. Without room to think, you lose the ability to logically weigh available options, and you miss out on opportunities.

FREE

Human nature is to seek the path of least resistance, to survive. By shining light on these natural mental roadblocks that are standing in your way, you can become conscious of how they are limiting you and then take ownership of moving them. Awareness is an invaluable tool in getting out of your own way, and through it you can see how fear drives large portions of our behavior when we do not realize it's there.

Regardless of whether your instinct may be to freeze before resistance, to turn and run, or to senselessly pound at it, the first step to moving forward is realizing what your reaction to the obstacle is. Awareness is a powerful thing when combating mental roadblocks.

You will be uncomfortable when you pursue "big, hairy, audacious goals" (BHAG),[2] regardless of when and why you pursue them. If you want to stay outside the box and try new things, fear

---

[2] The term "big, hairy, audacious goals" (BHAG) was originally coined by Jim Collins and Jerry Porras in their book *Built to Last: Successful Habits of Visionary Companies* (New York: HarperBusiness, 1994).

will be present. It's not a matter of pushing fear deep down so it no longer bothers you or trying to make it go away.

Seeing that it is there is the first step in learning how to coexist with it. The next step is getting comfortable within that coexistence.

Those who figure out how to bring fear along for the ride on this road trip of life are those who end up making the most progress toward their goals throughout their lifetime. And they are also the most likely to be living the life they envisioned.

TAKING FEAR ALONG FOR THE RIDE

Fear can be an odd comfort when we are uncomfortable. It fills those spaces of uncertainty tightly and becomes an easy crutch to rely on when making decisions. Understand that just because you are scared, it doesn't mean you shouldn't pursue your goal.

The more experience you have with a specific fear, the easier it becomes to cope with.

A good portion of pain is the fear of what it will do to us. It's the anticipation that's crippling. Once we have experienced the pain and know what to expect, it's not as bad as the moments leading up to it. Then it is not so scary the next time we have to endure it.

Why not cope with fear by getting comfortable with it just being along for the ride? The more often you allow space for it, the easier it will get to cope with and the less likely it is to hinder you from pursuing your goals.

Remember, you never really have to start over when it comes to coping with fear. Even if something goes wrong the first time, the next time you try, you will start with the knowledge you gained. Knowledge cannot be taken away; you learn regardless of the result. Even if all you learn is what it would feel like to try, you have still made progress in getting comfortable with the process.

The next time you are going after something you really want and your survival instincts try to take over, determine if you're reacting because you need to do so to survive or if your knuckle-dragger brain just can't tell the difference between a saber-toothed tiger and this "risk" you have decided to take because it's a new condition. I put "risk" in quotations because the level of the risk doesn't really matter. Any new input can trigger these instincts. Once you realize you are not facing a life-and-death threat, accept that those feelings you are experiencing are simply trying to help you.

The less you fight your feelings, the less they fight back.

So allow space for the feelings of anxiety and trepidation.

I like to view fear as a friend that's along for the ride. We're in a car, going on a road trip, snacks and drinks packed in a cooler in the back seat, windows down, music on in the background. Fear sits next to me in the front passenger seat, but we are going to be taking this trip together, and I am the one in control.

Author Elizabeth Gilbert paints this picture incredibly well in her masterful work *Big Magic*.[3] She says, "If I can relax, fear relaxes, too." She then goes on to explain that she allows her fear a seat in the car because by making space for it, she finds she is more likely to complete the trip. But she tells her fear "...my dear old familiar friend, you are absolutely forbidden to drive."

So the trick is to take fear along for the ride. The faster you can get comfortable with sitting with that uncertain tension, the more aware you become of its limitations, which enables you to accept that discomfort. Now, instead of freezing, running away, or pounding back at what scares you, you can continue making progress toward your goal.

---

[3]   Elizabeth Gilbert, *Big Magic: Creative Living Beyond Fear* (New York: Riverhead Books, 2015).

QUICK TIPS

» You are human; fear is natural. Do not allow your knuckle-dragging Neanderthal brain to take over when faced with fear. Use your awareness of it to keep moving forward.

» A good portion of pain is the anticipation of it. The more comfortable you get with that fact, the more efficiently you can move through it. Get comfortable with being uncomfortable.

» It's so easy to take the path of least resistance and not do something because it seems too risky, especially if so many around you are stagnant and may only offer criticism if they see you trying. Take the intentional path toward your goal regardless of the resistance.

The next time you set out to do something big or different, or even just simply try something new, and you feel that tension welling up and your head says, "Woah, there..." accept that it's your instincts working to help you survive. Also recognize that moving forward in that discomfort is how to thrive. This is what sets apart those that accomplish big, hairy, audacious goals from those who don't; they understand that sitting in that discomfort is part of the process that enables them to move past these self-imposed default limitations.

Take the next step and accept that discomfort and fear are part of the process.

Pain is temporary; regret sticks.

CHAPTER 5

BEARING

WHEN I WAS IN THE MARINE CORPS, land navigation was a critical part of combat training. Understanding how to determine where you were and where you needed to go using topographic maps and physical land attributes were survival skills. While a lot of emphasis was placed on getting to the end point, where you needed to go, I quickly learned that figuring out where I was starting from, getting my bearing accurately, was actually more important.

One day, while in the woods during a training exercise with a blindfold tightly around my eyes, I felt the tap on my shoulder signaling me to stop, then I heard footsteps walking away in the brush—no doubt, getting out of earshot in the wrong direction to mislead me. I was waiting for the distant blare of the bullhorn that would signal the start of the exercise.

A few moments later, the bullhorn sounded. I pulled off the blindfold, opened my eyes, and crouched down. The test had begun. Considering the penchant I had developed for land navigation, I wasn't going to let myself be taken out for idiotically standing while my eyes focused. As I swiftly made my way to a nearby tree, staying as low and quiet as I could, I quickly noticed I was on a downward slope that rose up again roughly five meters away. A good amount of dried leaves and brush had gathered in the space between the "V" formed by the hills. I leaned against the tree and pulled out my map and compass. The sloping was doing me favors, but it would still take a few precious moments to figure out where I was.

I focused solely on getting my bearings; I needed to make sure I accurately determined where I was starting from. The map didn't have a "You are here!" star. I had to figure out where I was in order to map the route to where I needed to go. I also had to account for the landscape I was traveling in and decide the route that would best keep me hidden since I did not know where the "enemies" were along the way.

For the prior three weeks, I had been participating in a combat-training simulation. This moment was the culmination of the land navigation portion of it. Each week kept us in the same simulation but focused on a specific aspect of training that we had to test out of to advance. I had really fallen for land navigation and enjoyed trekking through the wilderness day and night, learning topography, latitude and longitude rules, and how to accurately calculate routes with very limited tools. This test consisted of being led out into the woods from a random point on a back road and then being left there with a compass and a topographical map that included the area but covered a much larger space. We had to make our way to a specific finishing area within a certain time frame in order to pass. There would be "enemies" in the tree lines, meant to distract us and make us have to reconfigure our routes under pressure in order to stay undetected.

Throughout our training in land navigation, a lot of emphasis was placed on making it to the end goal. It was driven into us how important it was to be accurate in finding the finish so that we got within the boundary and could pass the test. We were all Marines and selected to be in this specialized training simulation. Remaining calm in high pressure was easy enough, but many struggled with the calculations under a time crunch because they failed to see the importance of figuring out where they were starting from with each drill. The finish point coordinates would be provided to us, but where we would be dropped in the woods changed every time.

Without taking time to determine where you're starting from, it is impossible to accurately calculate the route to get to the finish and also take the next correct steps. We may have all undergone the same training, but we all had different life experiences and different talents, and we were all starting from different places in the wilderness. When we got left in the woods, the only thing we had in common was that we possessed the same physical tools to figure out the puzzle.

The ones who passed the training and made it to the correct finishing point were the ones who took action quickly without wasting time questioning their instincts or trying to cheat the test. The ones who questioned inevitably ended up taking so long to do their calculations that they were discovered by the "enemy" and never made any significant progress. Those who tried to cheat the test focused on following the direction in which they thought they heard the monitor walk after the monitor led them to the start point. Of course, the monitors tried to flesh out the cheaters by simply walking away in the wrong direction. So trying to cheat or take a shortcut led them away from the finishing point.

Regardless of where you start from, you can reach your desired goal. You just need to calculate the route as best you can and then actually walk it. Get your bearings and start from wherever you are, wherever that may be.

What if this chapter in your life is the wilderness? Do you want to spend it crouched behind the tree, analyzing or waiting for someone to come get you? Or would you prefer to take steps toward where you want to go?

Come on, friend, let's get going.

STARTING WITH "NOTHING"

Becca looked at me intently, ready to take notes in the spiral notebook laying in front of her. The whirring of the coffee grinder behind me coupled with the smell of the fresh beans was nearly soothing as I thought through how delicately I may want to treat this meeting. Becca had been working for me for a few months and had a lot thrown at her in that time frame. She had to adapt quickly, but different aspects of her life were changing too. She was growing as a person, and her eyes were opening to possibilities she had not been aware of previously. In her administrative role, she worked closely with me on a day-to-day basis and seemed eager to go to meetings and site visits with me in order to learn about the many different facets of the business. Today, she had jumped at the opportunity to accompany me to see a home I was considering as an investment property. We walked the home, and afterward, I took her to one of my favorite coffee shops to review my thought process so she could really learn from the experience.

I talked to Becca about location, size, price, and the two factors that made me not want that specific home (more on these later). She scribbled intently while I slapped back my espresso. I could have left it at that. I had spent considerable time, effort, and money learning those things I freely handed her. I love teaching and training my team, but this wasn't a realm of her job responsibilities. Plus, it was still a workday, and I still had an arm's length of things to work on to finish it. However, I recognized how genuinely she appreciated what I was sharing with her, so I asked, "Would you like to know how to actually start though?" Her eyes widened and she smiled and nodded eagerly as "Yes" quickly tripped out of her mouth. "Ok, flip to a new page," I replied gingerly.

I told her to write out all her debts first, as long as she was comfortable with me seeing them. She reassured me she was fine, wrote down the balance of her car loan and the monthly payment, then looked up at me.

I said, "Is that everything?"

She nodded.

Becca, in her midtwenties and a Phoenix native raised by first generation parents, didn't have the privilege of learning extensively about money management. However, unlike so many others her age or younger who have much more debt after being bombarded with credit card offers and encouraged to buy things with money they don't have, Becca only had a very reasonable car note. I was proud of her restraint.

Becca rents an apartment, does not have VA Loan eligibility, and wants to own her own house. So I helped her lay out all of the variables impacting her ability to do that. She needed to be able to qualify for a price point within her budget; she would need a minimum 3.5 percent down payment in order to avoid relying on the availability of down-payment assistance programs; and she would need a stable work history.

Her first priority needed to be savings, so we calculated what she needed to save in total.

Then we sat at that table and outlined her monthly budget, including a line item for savings. Savings would be treated like a bill that needed to be paid instead of saving what was left over after monthly expenses. That way, we ensured Becca saved a specific and consistent amount each month.

Based on the plan we created, Becca would be able to begin the home-buying process in eighteen months. We made her a checklist where she could check off each month that she "paid the savings bill" and see the progress she was making.

She was giddy with excitement and couldn't wait to start chipping away at this progress. Because she was so excited, Becca was also motivated to play with her numbers and see if she could reach her benchmark faster. So she deeply considered which expenses she could cut back on and asked for ideas for opportunities to earn additional income.

Mapping her route not only provided Becca with the steps she needed to take to reach a goal that had once seemed far-fetched to her, but it also motivated her to consider even bigger goals and use excitement to focus on what she wanted to achieve.

I looked Becca in the eye and told her she may not always be excited by the process, that making progress on her savings may feel dull as time goes by, but that every time she checked a month off her list, she should see it as a win and reflect on how good it felt to make this plan.

As you can see, Becca started with "nothing": no debt other than a car loan, and a little money in savings. Of course, Becca has a stable job, a stable place to live, and reliable transportation (this is not meant to take those things for granted, since not everyone has them). Becca's plan shows that you do not have to start from an advanced place with tons of money or connections in order to map a route. There is no predetermined list of things you must possess or attributes you must have to get started working toward your goals, your vision.

STARTING WITH DEBT

Debt has come as a regular obstacle in this book because it is a frequent one. There are many experts out there with varying degrees of experience that have made fortunes out of telling consumers how to get out of debt. So there are a plethora of plans you could follow and services you could pay for to assist you with overcoming debt.

In my experience, the most effective plan for tackling debt is the most sustainable one. Meaning the one that you are most likely to follow. Who better to determine which plan you're most likely to stick with than you?

When you are starting with debt, your vision usually involves being free from it or alleviating it so you can accomplish your vision. No matter what your vision is—to have more disposable income, to have more investments that create income opportunities, or to travel more freely—in order to move forward, you need to face debt head-on in some form. To do so, start by outlining your debts, noting the balances, the monthly payments, and the interest you are being charged on the balance. You must have these variables in front of you to map them into your route to overcome debt.

Now that you have your list, you have some self-evaluation to do. If you do not take time to reflect on how you got here, you are likely to end up right back in the same spot. Trapped in a cycle, one step forward, two steps back...perhaps without realizing it.

That's where DeAnna was. She used her credit card for most purchases. She always got excited about her credit card companies' cash-back program on certain purchases. DeAnna didn't consider herself the typical consumer because she only purchased things she would otherwise pay for with her debit card, so she wasn't frivolous. She had a few thousand dollars on the highest-balance credit card but just enough in savings to pay that one nearly off if she wanted to. So, she felt like she was in a great spot, working the system.

DeAnna had consumer credit debts linked to specific stores as well, but they offered a slight discount for having those cards, so again she felt like she was using the system to her advantage. She had a low balance on her car after owning it for nearly the length of the original car loan. DeAnna frequently posted on her social media accounts about the investments she was making using popular apps. She also publicly shared her plans to buy a Tesla. DeAnna is active duty in the military, and her dream is to get out and become a financial influencer so she can be paid through social media content based on her successes.

However, DeAnna was trapped. Month by month, she would charge purchases she "knew" she could pay off. When the bills came in, she was attached to the money she had saved, so she would pay little more than the minimum required but not enough to make progress toward paying off each debt. As a result, her credit card debt had accumulated gradually. Meanwhile she had not been putting aside money for savings because she felt like she had enough. In an effort to build her social media following, DeAnna illogically focused on her stock market investments, a move she thought would appeal to her followers, and added leftover money to her investment accounts each month.

It is clear that DeAnna was making no real progress. Even though she felt like she had enough in savings, the moment anything happened, she would just put it on credit, like when she needed a new set of tires. She was not making intentional decisions or following a route to get to her goal. Instead, she was just cycling through the same pattern over and over. The interest she was being charged on the credit card balances outweighed any money she was making using the investment apps. Therefore, she was never getting ahead, although it may have seemed like she was to her followers.

If I were to push her to follow a plan to pay down debt and make progress toward her goals, she might start, but would she sustain her momentum or just fall back into the same pattern?

To accomplish her vision, DeAnna needs to see the pattern she is in and choose to change it.

You, too, need to see the traps you may have fallen into and choose to move forward differently. You need to stop using debt in order to get out of it.

When you're ready to make that choice, the next steps become easier.

Take your debts, including balances, payments, and interest rates, then order them in a list from smallest balance to highest balance. Do not include auto loans or mortgage loans. If you have balances that are similar, put down the one with the higher minimum payment first. Disregard anything but the balance for right now.

Now look at your savings account. Write down how much you have there and in any other accounts (including investment/ stock accounts).

Next, write out your income and all revolving expenses, including the total.

Now that you have gathered all the information, decide the minimum amount you need to have in savings in order to no longer use your credit card, barring a catastrophe. A good amount to start with is $1,500.

If you **do not have $1,500 in savings** yet, your focus would be to get there first before moving forward. Remember, the benchmark to meet here is to free your income from extra monthly credit card payments so you can leverage it more effectively to meet your goals. We will come back to building up more savings once you have freed yourself from this trap.

If you have more than $1,500 in savings, start applying your savings overage to your lowest-balance credit card. If you are able to pay it off and still have funds left over, apply those funds to the next balance on your list.

You will quickly make big progress in a short amount of time. Now those minimum monthly payments you were required to put toward the card(s) will be paid off, and you can lump that money into the amount you pay toward the balance of the next-lowest card balance on the list.

Moving forward, make the minimum required payments on all credit card debts, except the one with the lowest balance. For that card, apply any excess funds you can toward the balance each month (in addition to paying the required minimum). As you pay off a balance, lump the amount you were putting toward that balance with the minimum required payment you were putting toward the card with the next-lowest balance.

For example, if you were paying $135 per month to pay off the credit card with the lowest balance and paying $35 per month minimum required payment toward the credit card with the second-lowest balance, then once you've paid off the card with the lowest balance, pay $170 ($135 + $35) per month toward paying of the card with the second lowest balance. You are used to paying the bill anyway, so use it to your advantage.

Many well-known financial gurus talk about paying off debt like this in their own styles. For the purposes of ensuring you get the most leverage possible, I recommend you continue this pattern until the only debt you have left is a car loan (and mortgages if you have them).

Once your debts are paid down, you have effectively freed up your income to apply it to making progress toward your vision. This is a huge benchmark to overcome in your route and may take some time.

TRENDS AREN'T FRIENDS

These days, investing in the stock market is a trend. There are multiple apps that enable you to toss in any amount you please, and it's popular to post screenshots of all your "gains." But how are you ever getting ahead? Maybe you luck out and "make" $200 in the stock market using an app on your phone that just enables you to invest whatever amount rounds your purchases up to the nearest $10 mark. You feel super amazing. Meanwhile, you've paid

$250 in credit card interest from carrying credit card balances you could have paid off with that "invested" money.

Even more likely, look how much more quickly you can "make $1,000" by following this path versus tossing money toward an investment account. If DeAnna made an above-average yield of 13 percent annually and she invested somewhere between $50 to $250 per month, it would take her two to three years to earn roughly $900 on her investments. But within six months, she freed up over $1,000 of her own money, money that she now has every single month, which she can then invest toward her dream future.

In other words, she was investing random small amounts, and yes, overall, she made an above-average return throughout the time she had the account, but it wasn't giving her a gain anywhere near what she got by maximizing her own income through paying off debt. Plus, she will have the freedom of disposable income (since she was living before without this money while paying it toward debts), and she can leverage it to make big progress toward her goals.

Paying off debt to secure better stability in your finances is not the trendy path these days. But it is the more effective way to maximize your income so that you can make progress to meet your goals.

FRAMEWORK

You learned in previous chapters how to figure out where you want to go; that is your vision. Now you have learned how to map your route, how to connect two points on a map in a tangible (and realistic) way. You start by laying out what you have—this is getting your bearings and determining your starting point. The framework is how to determine your route and set the benchmarks that will guide you along the way.

No matter where you are starting from, even if you have more variables to consider, you can still map your route using this guidance.

1. Know where you want to end up: define your vision.
2. Get your bearings: see where you are starting from by laying out all of the variables impacting you.
3. Connect the dots: determine those specific benchmarks you need to reach, just like light posts guiding your way.

QUICK TIPS

» You've already learned the importance of determining your vision, where you want to go. Now, lay out all the variables impacting your ability to get there: each debt, savings, income, expense, and any requirements necessary to create benchmarks that will enable you to achieve your goal (like prequalifying to purchase a home or certification for that dream job).

» Free up your income to make the most effective progress toward your goals by paying off debt strategically.

» Despite what limitations you may feel because of where you come from, you can start making progress. Understand how to fill in your framework first, and then map your route.

We all have different challenges we've faced, different life experiences. Regardless of where you may be starting from, this framework is a common tool that anyone can use to map out their route and make progress toward their desired goal.

Just like a book, life tends to fall into chapters. This chapter of your life may be one where you have been stuck in the wilderness, either frozen behind a tree or wandering around waiting for a path to present itself.

How this chapter closes is solely up to you.

CHAPTER 6

THE APPROACH

MARY DREAMED OF BEING A NURSE. In high school she took advanced placement courses and volunteered her spare time at the local hospital. During her junior year of high school, she began taking college courses to start working on general education credits so she could get ahead and be more competitive when applying to nursing school. Her longtime boyfriend, Leo, was super supportive and had ambitions of his own in the medical field. He planned on joining the Air Force to work in medical and get education benefits, which would enable him to gain the necessary experience and the ability to pay for advanced education requirements for his dream of getting into radiology.

Mary and Leo had talked extensively about their future together and ultimately decided they wanted to get married.

Mary received her acceptance letter to nursing school the same day Leo received his date for departure; they took it as a sign and got engaged that day.

Not long after high school, Leo went off to Basic Military Training (BMT) for the Air Force. Mary knew she would soon be a military spouse and did not know where they would end up living, so she decided not to start nursing school until Leo got his orders. She knew she would likely need to reapply, but she was scared that if she started nursing school now, she wouldn't do well. So she enjoyed a summer with her friends and family, soaking in every moment she could, knowing she would soon be leaving behind everything she knew.

After completing BMT, Leo was to report straight to tech school for training in his specific job field before reporting to his first duty station. Mary had expected to be able to go with him but found out she would not be able to accompany him. Since she didn't know where Leo would be assigned after that stop, Mary was worried that if she took a job only to quit soon after, it would look bad for her. And it was too late to start a semester of college courses.

Leo received his first duty assignment while in tech school and would need to report there immediately upon graduation. Mary would be responsible for moving herself halfway across the country to follow Leo. With her parents' help, she managed, and soon after arriving, Leo and Mary got married and moved into a nice townhouse.

Each day, Leo went to work and Mary stayed home. She continued to think about applying for nursing school, but she was scared that if she started nursing school right now, it would be too stressful and she wouldn't do well. She considered enrolling in college to continue toward an associate's degree and get some general education out of the way for her bachelor's, but she was worried that it would be a waste of time since she really wanted to do a proper full-length nursing program.

They weren't making as much money as they had expected with Leo's service. Finances were getting tight, so Mary looked into getting a job to fill the gaps. She knew she wanted something related to the medical field even if it was just a job in a medical building. Although she browsed online, she never applied for a job because she was convinced she was underqualified for the jobs she wanted and didn't want to risk being rejected.

The obligations of adult life continued to close in around them, so they decided to move into on-base housing and give up the townhouse they had been renting. Mary was able to make some friends who stayed home during the day so she didn't feel as isolated being home all alone. She talked regularly about wanting to go to nursing school, but she didn't look at school options, fearful it wouldn't work out. Occasionally, she would check available jobs in the medical field, but, again, she was worried she didn't have enough experience to apply and didn't want to risk being rejected.

Leo was very focused at work, and they got into a steady routine. They had enough money to get by, leaving enough to go out with friends each month or buy the latest video game. However, they weren't really saving. They had obtained a credit card for emergencies; they felt grown up and felt that they had their lives together.

Five years later, Mary still had not reapplied for nursing school or worked a job in the medical field. She continued to be too afraid to take the risk to try, too afraid she would fail.

HOW TO DECIDE IF SOMETHING IS A GOOD CHOICE FOR YOU

The term "risk management" sounds very official and like it could only be reserved for big-time investors, fund managers, or maybe accountants. But risk management is something everyone experiences every day. If you look both ways before crossing a street, you are weighing the risk. If you google reviews for a business before you use it, you are weighing the risk. If you ask a friend how something was before you try it, you are weighing the risk.

That knuckle-dragging Neanderthal loves thinking about risks, going back and forth, concentrating on what could go wrong. Our more conscious selves crave a crystal ball to tell us what will happen in the future before making a decision. To what extent you feel that back-and-forth anxiety, or crave the certainty of knowing, fluctuates based on the level of risk involved and your own risk tolerance.

So what makes some people more open to taking the big chances and others so scared? I would argue that being exposed to the feeling of taking a chance on something that scares you, experiencing what it feels like if it does or doesn't work out, makes you more willing to take a chance in the future. In fact, the times when it doesn't work out are more valuable because in surviving these experiences, you become less afraid to take the next risk. This is where resilience is built. Some personality traits play into your comfort level with risk, but ultimately, these traits only define your comfort in the action of taking the risk; they impact your willingness but are not the sole reason why you do not go for something you want.

Fear is the biggest culprit when you consider taking a risk. Emotion drives the decision more often than logic, as we discussed when we talked about the importance of taking fear along for the ride. You can now find comfort as you do that, because you can manage risk in a logical way. Here's how.

You understand the relationship between balance and gravity, especially when coupled with unstable forward motion. That sounds scientific, but you know that if you run too fast down a steep hill, you'll probably trip and skin a knee, right? So your fear is the emotion that you feel when you consider running down the hill, but logic also plays a role as you weigh the risk.

Is it worth it to run really fast down a hill, knowing I might get injured? Is what I'm running toward worth the potential injury? The reward for getting down the hill quickly may far outweigh the risk of injury. It depends on the answers to the following questions:

» What is at the bottom of the hill (your vision)?
» Why do I want to get to the bottom of the hill (your motivation)?
» What do I have to do to get there (your route)?
» What could hurt me (your risk)—is it worth it?

As you see, you can logically decide which risks are worth taking. That is the best way to make these types of decisions.

When it comes to making an investment, whether that investment is in money or time, it's often difficult to understand how to determine which choice will result in a skinned knee and which choice is worth the tumble and the potential reward. If you continue to rely on emotions to make decisions along your route, you will inevitably be pulled into that limiting Neanderthal frame of mind, and you will struggle to make real progress.

When you use logic to determine possible outcomes, decision-making becomes easier. You also discover your tolerance for risk, which will then inform future decisions.

WEIGHING RISK WITH PROPERTY

When you buy your first home, it is not a requirement to have defined your end goal or vision for the life you want to lead. Many people aren't exposed to how life-changing thinking about long-term goals can be until they've experienced bigger life events like buying a home. If you are starting from a place of owning a home, you may have already mapped a route, and you're either a little stuck on it, or you need more guidance regarding how to maximize your progress. It's also a likely possibility that when you purchased your home, you were just buying a place and didn't have a specific end goal in mind.

Regardless of which category you fall into, a home is a powerful asset to leverage toward your vision. The most common crossroads I find people facing is needing to move and not knowing the best option regarding their current home: rent, refinance, or sell.

Renting

When you rent out a home, you are keeping equity tied up in an asset in return for that asset generating income for you. The amount of money brought in from the home minus your expenses to keep it is your return on investment. Seasoned investors take this annual return and divide it into the original investment they made into the property to determine the percentage of return on investment they are getting on the property.

In other words:

$$\frac{(\text{Annual Income} - \text{Annual Expenses})}{\text{Original Out-of-Pocket Expenses}} = \text{Return on Investment}$$

This formula is very valuable in our decision-making process, but it fails to take into consideration the opportunity cost that results from keeping the amount you could make from selling the property tied up in the asset. For that reason, when you are deciding if a home you own is the right property to rent out, I recommend you calculate the formula as if you were buying the property again but investing the amount of equity you have in it.

In other words:

$$\frac{(\text{Annual Income} - \text{Annual Expenses})}{\text{Money You Could Get from Selling}} = \text{Return on Equity}$$

Calculating return on equity is the same concept as return on investment. You are just treating the equity you have in the home as if you invested it. This is valuable in decision-making because it shows you what that money is doing for you and helps you weigh if it's worth it to cash in this property for another opportunity.

Real estate is a tangible investment, making it a great hedge against inflation and other dangers in the marketplace. For me to consider letting go of a real estate investment, it would have to be either because my family needed access to the money or because a more lucrative real estate investment opportunity was available to me (and I needed the money from a current investment to take advantage of that opportunity).

For example, Cedrick and I purchased a property and lived in it for roughly two and a half years. We then rented it out and moved into a different home. After renting it out for over two years and owning it for roughly four and a half years, we were considering selling it. The market was expected to continue climbing, but with the appreciation we had in the home, I suspected the equity could be leveraged for better use elsewhere. I calculated our return on investment if we were to keep the property and our return on equity. Then I calculated what our return on investment would be if we were to put the money into another property. Because of this math, I was able to determine that our numbers would come out much better if we were to sell this property and split the equity from it into two smaller rental homes. Using the equity as down payments, we would lower our annual expenses while simultaneously increasing our annual income. We would also gain another appreciating asset since we could leverage one property into two.

On the other hand, sometimes the math just does not make sense. If your percentages are lower, it may be more favorable if you were to sell and reinvest the money into the market you are moving to.

In other instances, life events may interrupt your plans, and you won't be in a position to leave this kind of money sitting in a home, because your family needs it.

Even if you bought this home intending to rent it out one day, and that's just not possible anymore, understand that you are still starting from a position of having a home to leverage. You already made a decision that can earn you money. Good job.

Deciding to rent out a home can feel like an emotional decision, or one you need a crystal ball to make. But it isn't, because the above formulas don't take appreciation into consideration. Therefore, the property does not have to go up in value for it to be a good investment; it could go down in value and still be a good investment.

In other words, it does not matter how the home's value may increase or decrease in the future. Historically, rents (annual income) have stayed on a stable trend regardless of whether home values went down or not. Do not make the decision to rent based on the expectation that the home value will go up. Make the decision based on the numbers you know. Calculate your return on investment. If the result works for you and you are ok with the responsibility of continuing to maintain the home, go for it!

Refinancing

The subject of refinancing can be a land mine.

In my professional opinion, refinancing is only ever worthwhile if you intend to keep a property you currently own long term or if you need a method to leverage money out of a current property without selling it and the numbers make sense.

Yes, there is math for determining if refinancing is a good idea, regardless of why you may be considering it.

No, it is not as simple as saving some money on your monthly mortgage payment.

Refinancing can give you the ability to rent out a property but still access a good portion of the equity to use as you please. This sounds-to-good-to-be-true option is real, but it has costs associated with it.

When you refinance a mortgage, you are borrowing against the house again. The original loan is paid off by the new mortgage, and any remainder is paid out to you, if you elect to borrow more than what you owe on the property.

To illustrate, here's a rudimentary example that doesn't include moving costs and other variables.

Let's say I buy a house for $400,000, then five years later, the house is worth $500,000 and I owe $375,000. Although I owe a lower amount than when I bought the house, my mortgage payment is still the same because I agreed to a thirty-year fixed payment plan and I have twenty-five years left on that plan.

I could refinance this house for $375,000 with the same lender (or a new one), and my monthly payment would decrease, as long as I could get the same interest rate or lower, because I am borrowing a lesser amount of money but stretching it back out across thirty years.

Another option would be to refinance the house for $475,000. My monthly payment would likely go up due to the larger balance I would be borrowing, but I would get $100,000 cash to use however I would like and still owe $25,000 less than what the home is worth. Meaning that at the time I do the refinance, despite taking cash out of the investment, I would not be "upside down" on it (owe more than it is worth). Here's why:

>> $475,000 – $375,000 = $100,000 cash to me
>> $500,000 – $475,000 = $25,000 equity remaining in the home

In either option, the original mortgage is replaced by, known as refinanced by, the new mortgage.

When you refinance, you must pay closing costs, just like when you buy a home. The closing costs on a refinance are less than when originally purchasing a property because you are only required to pay the loan-related closing costs. Typically, lenders lump these costs into the new loan balance, but it does not change the fact that they are there.

If you are considering refinancing a property without taking cash out, your goal is most likely to reduce the monthly payment. I cannot tell you how often I have seen people get caught up in reducing their monthly payment, to the point where they are bragging about their refinance or their interest rate, without knowing the overall math of the experience. To determine if a refinance makes financial sense, use this formula:

$$\frac{\text{Total Closing Costs \& Fees for Refinance}}{\text{Monthly Savings}} = \frac{\text{Months BEFORE}}{\text{You Save Money}}$$

You can take this a step further and divide the resulting number by twelve to see how many years it will take for you to save money. If you sell before this time, then you will lose money as a result of refinancing.

Therefore, refinancing just to reduce your monthly payment is only worthwhile if you intend to keep the property longer than the time it takes for you to recover the cost. The exception to this rule would be if something has changed in your life since you bought your home and you are no longer able to afford your mortgage payment. Refinancing could be an option that allows you to stay in the home because it brings the mortgage payment to within your new budget.

If you are considering refinancing a property and taking out cash, you want to be very careful. Not only do you need to consider the cost of the refinance itself, but I would also recommend making sure the new mortgage payment would still work if you were to rent out the home. You can do this by calculating your return on investment and return on equity using the new figures (what the numbers would be if you were to refinance).

Even if you do not know whether you will rent it out in the future, you do not want to completely eliminate that possibility. If the market changes and you have to move for your job or other reasons, you may be in a position where you need to rent the property out for a while because you no longer have enough equity to sell.

If you need to refinance a property to free up enough of your VA Loan benefit to use it for buying your next primary residence, you still want to ensure that the costs of the refinance itself align with your plans for the property.

Before committing to the refinance, make sure:

>> the new mortgage payment fits into your budget;
>> you intend to own the home long enough for the cost to be worth it;
>> the new mortgage payment would still work if you were to rent out the home; or
>> you need to free up VA Loan eligibility, and your return on investment makes sense.

For example, if you only want to keep this home for six more months and then sell it, but it would take fifteen months to profit from the refinance, it may make more sense to just wait until you sell it before buying the next one with the VA Loan. In most cases I have seen, if you are advanced enough in your journey to be taking steps like this, the strategy with the property you are refinancing would be longer term, but that doesn't preclude you from needing to do your homework to make sure the decision is a sound financial one.

Selling

Sometimes a vision includes owning multiple properties as investments and wanting to have income from those properties as rentals. This can put you in a tough decision-making spot when it comes time to move because, by all accounts, the decision is made—rent out your current home!

But it's more complex than that. Maybe you have substantially more equity than you anticipated and you're moving out of state without plans to return. Maybe you're getting out of the military and moving to a place you intend on staying permanently. Maybe some life events have come up that could be relieved by selling your house and receiving the lump sum of its equity.

Selling your current home does not mean losing progress toward your vision of owning multiple properties. Stay focused on your vision, but understand that the path to get there may look different than you anticipate.

If the market you are going to is on an upward trajectory similar to what you have already experienced where you currently own your home, then it's likely a better idea to sell.

For example, Nate Cole was retiring from the military. He and his family were moving to an area near where they grew up and near to their extended family in Georgia. They owned their home in a Phoenix, Arizona, suburb and had always intended on renting it out. But when it came time to plan their transition, they realized they had much more equity in the Arizona home than they had anticipated. With that money, they could buy a dream home with a large down payment in Georgia, and their monthly payment would be much less than they were paying in AZ, leaving them with plenty of money to pad their savings during this big life shift. Although their vision had included owning multiple properties for additional income so they could live very comfortably, selling the home would give them that comfort without added stress or maintenance. So they decided it was a no-brainer for them to sell.

What you decide to do with a home will vary based on your vision and the progress you have made over the period of time you own it.

Here are the main factors that will determine which route to take regarding your current home as you are mapping your way to your vision:

> **Can you qualify to buy your next home without selling this one?** If you have to move and you cannot qualify to buy your next home without selling this one, consider if it is better to hold on to this home and rent at your new location for a while, or if it is better to sell

this one to buy the next home at the new location. If you do not have to move and you cannot qualify to buy your next home without selling this one, the math might tell you it is better to just stay put until you can qualify to buy the next home so that you can keep both.

» **Do you need the money from your current home in order to buy your next home?** (Even if you can qualify, you may still need the money from your current home.) If you do need the money from your current home, use the refinancing formula above to see if refinancing is a good option. If refinancing doesn't make logical sense, then it's time to weigh the same options in the previous bullet point, as if you could not qualify to buy the next home without selling your current property.

» **Are you able to qualify, don't need the money from your existing home, and don't have to move?** Decide if you want to rent out your current home and move into the next home or buy the next home to immediately rent out. This may impact what you decide to purchase and therefore when you will be able to take this step.

» **Have you considered how each option will impact your lifestyle?** Your vision is the goal, but think about the different ways that are available to accomplish it.

INFLATION

Generally, the cost of goods and services go up over time, decreasing the purchasing power of money. In other words, it takes more dollars to buy something now than it did five years ago. This is the principle of inflation.

It is critical for you to have a basic understanding of inflation if you want to have financial stability. Inflation impacts the cost of everything you need to survive and influences investment options predictably enough to give you the opportunity to thrive in times when inflation is high.

In July 2022, inflation was logged at 8.5 percent over the past year. That is the highest it has been since 1981. The general cost of consumer products went up more in one year than we have seen across the previous three to four years combined. This was a big jump, but the average consumer didn't see it coming. You felt the large jump at the gas pump first, then you noticed your grocery bill was more for the same products, and before you knew it, that income that had previously felt comfortable, or was enabling you to survive didn't feel like enough anymore, even though it didn't change. How far each dollar could get you is what changed.

So, if inflation just happens and we can't do anything impactful about it, why is it so critical to understand it? If we can't control it, then what can we do about it?

Inflation occurs every year, however the degree varies. Knowing it happens should incentivize you to look for ways to increase your income to a level above inflation. Too many consumers take to social media and their more personal social circles to complain about gas prices and the cost of groceries. Complaining won't make it go away, and regardless of what they may promise you, politicians cannot make it go away either.

The economy is cyclical, and in the specific cycle during which I'm writing this book, there are bottlenecked supply chains, shortages in trade labor, and international discord that have made goods more expensive to produce and move. This is happening during a time when consumers have more money in savings on average as a result of being pent up during the COVID-19 pandemic. When demand is high and supply becomes stunted, pricing on goods goes up, and service providers typically increase their prices to account for higher material costs.

These factors cannot all be muscled into remission overnight. So, historically, in periods of high inflation, governments try to slow down demand, giving supply an opportunity to rebound enough to slow down price increases. This is how we knew interest rates would be increasing, because raising rates to borrow money is a way to reduce demand.

When you understand inflation, you can predict what comes next.

Since inflation occurs every year, it makes sense to look at putting your money into opportunities that increase with inflation so that you don't lose value in terms of what your money is worth. You can make your income increase by adding side hustles (more work), and by adding additional avenues to protect your money.

STEPS TO TAKE TO PROTECT YOURSELF AGAINST INFLATION

There is a saying, "If you want to get ahead, get into drugs or real estate."

I wouldn't recommend drugs; I'd wager it's a rather tumultuous business. But there is a reason why Wall Street hedge funds have spent considerable money buying into the real estate market as inflation has increased. Typically speaking, real estate is a very safe way to protect yourself against inflation because, as we have established, when inflation goes up, the cost of living goes up...and what is a crucial component in living? Shelter, a.k.a. housing. So rents and housing prices increase with inflation.

Interest rates commonly go up during periods of high inflation, which impacts borrowing money to purchase homes and can scare some buyers out of the market. What experienced investors understand is that you buy the home and "rent the interest rate." Meaning once you buy the home, it's yours; you have secured a real estate investment that will provide you housing stability. As far as the interest rate goes, you can refinance the home later when interest rates come down.

Buying a home is meant to provide you with stability so that you can invest in your long-term future by owning something you have to pay for every month anyway (shelter). The housing security it provides comes from that predictable monthly payment that will not change at the mercy of someone else's whim (landlord). Landlords can decide not to renew your lease at any time or to increase the price at renewal. As long as you buy a home that fits into your monthly budget, you are buying yourself that security and paying toward an investment that will help protect you from inflation and give you multiple opportunities to accelerate your progress toward your goals.

If you aren't in a position yet to buy a home, don't stress. There are other ways to help protect yourself from inflation:

» Low-cost ETFs (exchange-traded funds): an exchange-traded fund is a basket of securities that tracks an underlying index. It contains multiple stocks and bonds, giving investors diversity in one place. The S&P 500 is an ETF that is a known favorite for Warren Buffet, the famous billionaire "Oracle of Omaha." You can open an account through etrade.com and purchase ETFs, but be sure you are only using money you do not expect to need over the next five years. You can sell and pull the money out at any time, but you would not want to do that and lose your position unless you were investing in something that would return a higher rate over the long term.

» Treasury inflation-protected securities (TIPS): a type of US Treasury bond, TIPS are indexed to inflation in order to explicitly protect investors from inflation. Twice a year, TIPS pay out at a fixed rate. The principal value of TIPS changes based on the inflation rate, and so the rate of return includes the adjusted principal. TIPS come in three maturities: five-year, ten-year, and thirty-year. You can buy bonds through treasurydirect. com or buy these securities in the form of ETFs. These you cannot sell prior to maturity without a penalty of losing some of the interest you have earned.

Remember, any investment that helps protect you from inflation is most impactful long term. These are all meant to be longer-term investments. If you sit and watch them move every day and move your money in and out of them, you will not have consistency in fighting inflation. There are plenty of investments suited for short-term movement that you could look into once you have mapped your route and taken the critical first steps toward your goal.

If you start investing in stocks like this prior to paying down debt, as we reviewed in the previous chapter, you are not getting ahead. During periods of higher inflation, interest rates increase. If you have an interest rate that is not fixed, it will be impacted by inflation. Meaning your credit card balance is being charged more in interest, so if you make money through a stock or bond, it is a wash because you are also paying more to carry debt. Fixed interest rates, like those you may have on auto and home loans, are not impacted by rising rates during inflation. So it is critical to focus on decreasing consumer debt balances first.

DON'T SETTLE

I sat on the edge of the cold folding chair in the third row. I had been gifted a ticket to attend the National Achievers Conference in Phoenix. Headline speakers for the event were Robert Herjavec, Gary Vaynerchuk, and Tony Robbins. I could not believe I would get to see these people in person who I had watched on YouTube so many times. It's been four years since that day, and I remember moments of it, but there is one moment that stands out most clearly and one I have thought about regularly.

Robert Herjavec, who is a highly recognized businessman known most commonly for his appearances on Shark Tank, said, "Treat your money like each dollar is a soldier. Your goal is to deploy your soldiers out into the world to recruit more soldiers for your cause. If you leave them in the barracks, they can never accomplish anything for you."

So many people in the military sit on the sidelines the entire time they are in the service because they cannot predict when they may have to move or deploy, or they figure they have a lot of time left before they have to think about life outside of the military.

For example, they want to wait until they retire from the military before buying their first home because then they won't have to worry about a house when they know they will need to move every few years.

But time will pass regardless of what you are doing with it.

If time will pass whether you buy a home or not, why not take a "risk" and send your soldiers out? Why not invest in yourself so that you can spend that time making progress toward something that has the ability to pay you back later?

QUICK TIPS

» Take a step back and make sure you are intentional about weighing risk and not making an emotional decision rooted in fear. The more practice you get in making decisions using logical variables, the more you will get to know your risk tolerance and the more progress you will make.

» The value of money goes down over time. The tighter you hold on to money, the more you close yourself off to making more of it. Taking risk by investing logically for your situation is mathematically less risky than hoarding your money long term.

» Deciding how to best leverage a home can feel like a highly emotional decision, or one you need a crystal ball to make. This is not the case. Use the formulas I provided to know your numbers and make a financial decision based on those numbers. They will help you make progress toward your vision.

You can never get back your time. Spend it trying to take intentional steps toward your vision. You could feel limited by your job, but if you don't use what time you have to make progress, you'll never be free from the cycle you resent.

If you sit on the sidelines crippled by a tendency to make emotional decisions, you will automatically fail to reach your goals simply because you didn't try. If you never take any risk to achieve your goals, then you will have to live with never knowing if it would have been worth the risk to get there.

When you calculate risk, you give yourself the tools you need to determine which path to take. You set yourself up for success. And you make it easier to achieve that success.

Logically evaluate the variables; tolerate risk by managing it intentionally. Go after your vision. I would be willing to bet that living in your vision is well worth the risk you may need to take to get there; otherwise it wouldn't be a dream.

CHAPTER 7

LUG NUT

DAWSEY WAS ACTIVE DUTY IN THE AIR FORCE, living less than paycheck to paycheck, when he met Juliet. In fact, he was dangerously close to having to choose which bills he paid every month. When they began dating, he didn't want Juliet to know that he was in such an unattractive financial state, so he went into further debt taking her to dinner, taking her to the movies, and never allowing her to pay, even when she wanted to. Within a couple months of dating, Dawsey needed to choose which bills he paid because there wasn't enough money to cover everything. He was deep in various debts and terrified Juliet would find out and want nothing to do with him. Dawsey constantly felt on edge and was sinking into depression, propelled further by anxiety.

One day, Dawsey and Juliet decided to go to Walmart to buy some groceries to make lunch together and watch their favorite show at Dawsey's place. They got excited walking the aisles deciding what they would make. At the checkout stand, Dawsey swiped his card to pay for their items and it was rejected. His heart sank and his stomach turned into a bundle of knots.

The cashier politely said, "Oh this darn thing, it is always messing up on us. Try again, honey."

Dawsey cracked what smile he could muster and held his breath as he swiped again, hopelessly knowing the likely outcome. "Rejected" flashed on the screen again. Dawsey wanted to melt into the floor; he just stared at the machine, willing it to magically tell him his payment was "accepted." A little receipt generated from the cashier's stand, and Dawsey hated the look the cashier gave him. He knew what she would say, and he knew it didn't matter because no other card would work.

The cashier said, "Do you have another card, honey?"

Juliet hadn't thought much of the interaction before this moment and perked up her head at the question.

Dawsey looked at Juliet's concerned face and said, "No. I'm sorry." He was sure he was about to be rejected just like his credit card because the well had run dry, and based on previous experiences with women, he knew what that meant. And this rejection would hurt deeply because Dawsey was convinced he wanted to marry Juliet.

Then something magical happened. Juliet smiled and although Dawsey couldn't be sure, he didn't think it looked like pity.

Juliet turned to the cashier and said, "Shoot! I forgot to bring my wallet in. Could you hold these bags for us while we go get it?" She turned back to Dawsey and laced her fingers with his, leading him out the automatic doors.

Dawsey was ashamed and watched the pavement as they walked to his truck. He figured Juliet was just being nice and would wait until they got back to his place to end things.

They got in the car and Juliet turned to him and said, "I'm sorry I left my wallet in my car back at your apartment. Do you mind running us over for me to get it?"

Dawsey couldn't hold it in anymore and told her everything.

She listened, nodding occasionally with warmth and understanding. When he finished, she looked at him for a moment and said, "It's okay. I'll help you figure it out if you want."

He smiled, relief washing through him. He had been so worried that Juliet would discover his financial problems and so frustrated knowing he had screwed up, so he didn't feel like he deserved her. Yet she responded kindly and confidently, knowing the load that had weighed him down for so long could be resolved.

After getting Juliet's wallet and paying for the groceries, they sat down and outlined Dawsey's debts. Juliet had ideas that Dawsey hadn't considered, and the fact that she cared enough to help motivated him to take the action his hopelessness had clouded him from seeing.

A few months later, Dawsey and Juliet got married and moved into Juliet's apartment because it was cheaper than Dawsey's. It was smaller and not as nice but would give them more elbow room as they worked together to get ahead and make a better life. With both of their incomes and by selling things they didn't need, they were able to start making progress toward getting out of debt, though the road ahead looked like it would be very long. Dawsey couldn't remember the last time he had felt such hope and confidence.

Soon, Juliet became pregnant unexpectedly, which was incredibly stressful because it seemed like the expense of caring for that child would derail the progress they had made. But they were committed.

When the baby came, Juliet couldn't work anymore because childcare cost equaled her income at the time. It felt like they'd be going back to square one, but they had each other.

Dawsey worked hard to try to make rank (get promoted) while Juliet took care of the baby, managed their finances, and worked toward a degree to make her future job prospects brighter. They lived on a tight grocery budget of $60 per week for the two of them since baby expenses took priority.

Six years later, Dawsey and Juliet were not only debt free (except for their vehicles and mortgages), but they had money in savings, had invested money in the stock market, and owned three houses. Two were rented out, providing them with extra money above expenses. They automatically saved that income and earmarked it for each of the rental homes to offset any potential needs those homes might have. The home they lived in was one they loved, nestled in a quaint neighborhood of their dreams and within walking distance to a school just like the one they had envisioned their son would ultimately attend.

THE EIGHTH WONDER OF THE WORLD

Albert Einstein is attributed to have said, "Compound interest is the eighth wonder of the world. He who understands it, earns it; he who doesn't, pays it."

Compound interest is what you earn on interest you'd have already earned. The majority of smoke-pit or water-cooler conversations that revolve around interest are related to interest you are paying (like on your mortgage or your car). However, it is so easy to get caught up on costs and completely miss opportunities.

Interest is a beautiful thing. It is money you earn on money you invest, and it can compound on itself, meaning money you earned without investing time can also make you more money. For example, if you invest $1,000 and it earns 6 percent interest each year, you will have $1,060 at the end of the first year. At the end of the second year, you will have $1,123.60. So, not only did you earn the $60 on the initial $1,000 deposit, but you also earned $3.60 on the $60 interest. It's money you did not have to trade your time to make and that has the ability to make you more money.

» $1,000 initial deposit × 6 percent interest = $1,060 after one year
» $1,060 total after one year × 6 percent interest = $1,123.60 after two years since initial deposit
» $1,123.60 total × 6 percent interest = $1,191.02 after three years since initial deposit
» Total after six years = $1,418.52, assuming you make no other deposits or contributions to this investment

That equals 41.85 percent more money in your pocket that you did not have to work to earn for those six years. Of course, you want to continue contributing to your initial investment in order to amplify your earnings.

It's free money!

The younger you start investing, the more you can earn. As we learned in the last chapter, the numbers need to make sense though. Do not invest to make gains when you are paying interest on consumer debts. That would be like chasing your tail; you wouldn't be moving forward at all.

MORE THAN INTEREST

What is even more interesting (pun intended) is how this principle of compound interest can be applied to other areas. The book *Atomic Habits* by James Clear illustrates how tiny changes can produce remarkable results.[4] Think of it like this: if you leaned a two-by-four plank by your door, and every time you went through that door, you cut a notch from the plank with your pocketknife, eventually all that would be left are wood chips. The action of cutting a simple notch each day is easy, but the prospect of shredding down the whole board at once with only a pocketknife sounds maddeningly impossible.

What could shift in your life if you committed to reading ten pages each day after work on the subject of personal development? You could read 2,400 pages per year, even if you skip reading on weekends.

» 10 pages × 5 days = 50 pages per week
» 50 pages × 4 weeks = 200 pages per month
» 200 pages × 12 months = 2,400 pages per year

---

[4] James Clear, *Atomic Habits: An Easy & Proven Way to Build Good Habits and Break Bad Ones*, (New York: Penguin Random House, October 2019).

What could those pages teach you? Even if each week's pages only gave you a sentence worth of a new idea or understanding, that's forty-eight new personal development opportunities per year that you did not previously have.

Compounding habits can be dangerous if you are not intentional about forming them. When you are compounding, make sure you are compounding something good. Let's say you fall into the habit of coming home from work each day, making a box of mac and cheese, then plopping down on the couch to watch TV for four hours until you go to bed. That compounds into twenty hours and 4,375 calories per week just from that habit, and that is assuming no TV or excess calories on the weekend.

- » 4 hours watching TV × 5 days = 20 hours per week
- » 20 hours watching TV × 4 weeks = 80 hours per month
- » 80 hours watching TV × 12 months = 960 hours per year
- » 875 calories (one whole box of mac and cheese, and— let's be honest—who doesn't eat the whole box?) × 5 days = 4,375 calories per week
- » 4,375 calories × 4 weeks = 17,500 calories per month
- » 17,500 calories × 12 months = 210,000 calories per year

Now let's be clear. I like TV and love mac and cheese! But not enough to give up 960 hours per year I could be spending working toward my vision, and not enough to sacrifice my health by loading my body with cheesy goodness in excess.

Understanding this is life changing: simple choices you make each day can compound into powerful shifts toward where you dream of being or powerful locks to keep you in a cage of your own design.

Neither Dawsey nor Juliet came from money, not even from middle-class America. Their families did not have the ability to help or support them in getting to this point in their lives. But they had a vision of where they wanted to go together, and they were dedicated to taking action to get there.

There was not one huge or ground-breaking event that happened to Dawsey or Juliet. Their progress came through compounding action, along with the magic of compounding interest. They took time to learn how to compound intentional habits and how to multiply their money by using resources available to them, enabling them to earn more over time. They understood, especially with the predictability of military income rates, that they would not be able to earn their way ahead through work alone.

COMMODITIES

Housing is a commodity opportunity.

In other words, housing is a vehicle for wealth and investment. But it provides something rather unique that other commodities arguably do not—security.

Owning where you live gives you control over what color walls you see every day and the security of knowing you are not at the mercy of a landlord who could decide to raise the rent or not to renew your lease. It also guarantees you a place to live at a stable cost. So, as we learned when we discussed inflation, as the cost of living goes up, your housing cost remains the same.

Franklin D. Roosevelt said, "Real Estate cannot be lost or stolen, nor can it be carried away. Purchased with common sense, paid for in full, and managed with reasonable care, it is about the safest investment in the world."

And he was right. There is great value in assets that you can reach out and touch, like a house. But the most value comes in commodities we cannot replicate.

There is only one commodity that we can truly never get back: time.

Trade time for money so you can trade money for time: this is the loop you will be forever trapped in until you take steps to make money without trading time for it. A lot of people refer to this as "passive income." I do not like that term because income that you do not trade time for is still income that took action to create. Many times people mistake "passive income" as something that's a guarantee, a given without need for oversight, but it is still an income that needs to be set up and then managed to a degree that ensures it can properly compound toward your goals.

You need to install additional pathways to overcome the loop.

Dawsey and Juliet worked to pay down debt, and the moment they could qualify to use their VA Loan to buy a home at their duty station, they did. That's what ultimately started them on the path to owning three homes, one to live in and two to rent out.

QUICK TIPS

» Look for ways to multiply your income. If you are not in a position yet to be able to invest, then look for opportunities to take on an extra part-time job or side hustle that will not cost you anything to start.

» It is much easier to add something than to take it away. Start by adding one favorable habit to your daily routine, commit to it, and see what progress you can make in a month. For example, bringing lunch from home versus eating out (financial and health gain) or skipping lunch, which is unhealthy.

» Understanding the "time for money, money for time" loop should motivate the hell out of you to get out of it. I have a hard time believing anyone consciously wants their life to resemble that of a merry-go-round from which you can never get off.

You must continue doing the work that will enable you to make progress toward your goals. If you take consistent action over and over, there is no option but to make progress.

In the military, one loose lug nut can cost a life. In your life, one habit can entirely change your trajectory, making all the difference in where you end up.

CHAPTER 8

CHECKS

I LOOKED TO THE UPPER RIGHT of my computer screen and realized it was nearly 3:00 a.m. I was still in the clothes I'd worn during the day. Time had completely escaped me. For the past eight hours, I'd been sitting on my couch hunched over my laptop.

It took a moment for my eyes to focus on the living room around me. It was completely dark and quiet. My husband and son were asleep, and this was the second night I had stayed up all night working on the website.

I knew how important it was for business owners to have websites, but I couldn't afford to have a custom one built. I wanted to ensure my site contained tons of resources and forms and that it looked professional. The problem was that I had never built a website, and when I decided to figure out how to do it myself, I had absolutely no idea where to begin.

It just felt so hard.

I tried to straighten my back, make it pop, and take a deep breath because it felt like I hadn't breathed for hours. It felt impossible that I would ever be able to grow a business, especially when it was this difficult to build the website.

Thoughts swirling through my mind for what must have been hours were pressing in and taking over my ability to focus. *If no one ever sees this, it will have been a waste of time*, I thought. *What if I can't finish it? What if I can't make it?*

Time to get some sleep.

I closed the computer but didn't get up. I looked around the living room at the traces of my family: some toy cars on the floor; a little table and chair with paper and crayons from my toddler; a compressed pillow with the outline of my husband's head from when he fell asleep earlier trying to stay up to keep me company.

I felt like they were watching me. If I was just going to give up the time I'd spent on the website, if I couldn't build it, that time would have been wasted, time I could have spent with my family. For them, I didn't want to be a quitter. I also didn't want to have to spend the rest of my life thinking about how close I might have been to success if I just kept going and it all came together.

I sighed and looked at my to-do list. "Build Website" looked so unassuming on the page, but reality was completely different.

I had spent so much time working on it that I knew I must have made some progress, yet I could see nothing I could check off that would please the part of my brain hungering for meaning.

I flipped the spiral to the next page and wrote "Build Website" at the top. Then I tried to think about what was left to do. Not knowing the answer, I began listing everything I had already completed.

BUILD WEBSITE

- ☐ Watch a beginner video on how to get started
- ☐ Pick a platform
- ☐ Reserve a URL
- ☐ Outline what pages I want on the menu tab
- ☐ Determine my goal for the home page
- ☐ Write the welcome message for the home page
- ☐ Write the About section
- ☐ Pick photos for each page header
- ☐ Learn how to link pages to the menu

Suddenly I was feeling accomplished about what I had completed, and excited for what was to come. I was on a roll, so I wrote everything else I needed to do to get the website live.

- ☐ Fill content on each page

- ☐ Learn how to make the same footer on every page with contact information
- ☐ Make the footer
- ☐ Learn how to make a lead form for visitors to fill out
- ☐ Make the form and link it to every page.
- ☐ Test all links and make sure they work

I thought, *Okay, so you're more than halfway there.* I smiled. I could do this.

CHOW TO CHOW, SUNDAY TO SUNDAY

When I went through Marine Corps boot camp, it was a physically grueling undertaking, but the mental game was much more vital to getting through the hardship. I would tell myself, "It's just fourteen Sundays. I just have to make it to the next Sunday."

But when you are going through that kind of full-body and mind taxation, it's easier to digest the challenge of every day by breaking it down further. Since we didn't have watches and rarely knew exactly what time it was, the best way to break up the days was with the three chow times: morning, afternoon, and evening. We had a whole slew of things thrown at us before even making it to morning chow, and organized chaos drilled into us at night after evening chow, but breaking that up by mentally wiping the slate clean at each chow was a game changer. I liked to envision myself as checking each chow off on a calendar. So no matter how hard it was, I always knew—no matter what—that I was making progress.

We have talked about how the time will be passing anyway, so you might as well spend it making progress toward your goals. But there is another beautiful perspective in the sentiment that time will pass anyway, and it's that no matter how hard something may be, you will get through it.

I've given you the concepts you need to get started, and I've given you the tangible information you need in order to make decisions and go for it. You outlined your framework in Chapter 6. You defined your vision (where you want to end up). You got your bearings by laying out the variables impacting you. Now it's time to start connecting the dots. You need to learn how powerful unpacking your vision into a workable checklist can be and learn what you need to do it.

HOW TO CREATE EFFECTIVE CHECKLISTS

Here you are putting together the tangible plan of how you get to the top of the mountain, to your big goal, your beautiful vision in that picture you drew. You are going to take your benchmarks and unpack them into tasks you can accomplish that will enable you to reach those benchmarks. Just like a distance runner counting light posts to guide their way, you are making your light posts to guide your way.

If your big goal is to live a better lifestyle than you currently live, without having to work more to make it happen, then you have two goals:

1. To develop additional income opportunities.
2. To reduce unnecessary expenditures in order to maximize those opportunities.

Consistently and predictably replacing a $5,000 per month income without having to go to work sounds difficult. But when you break the process down into a checklist, you will see how generating the income is attainable.

Your benchmarks (in no particular order) could be the following:

- ☐ Obtain property to rent out, which will enable you to develop more income opportunities.
- ☐ Pay off debt to maximize the income you have.
- ☐ Work a low- to no-overhead side hustle to speed your progress.
- ☐ Invest in opportunities that historically have a stable return over time.

Now you unpack each one.

How can I buy rental property? Well, you need to be able to prequalify and have down-payment funds available. Or you could buy a home and live in it for a couple of years, then buy another home, move into the new home, and rent out the first one. This saves you down-payment funds because you'd be buying another primary residence. When you purchase a primary residence with VA Loan eligibility, you do not have to provide a down payment. Even if you are not able to use the VA Loan, down-payment requirements for a primary residence are much lower than if you were to buy a property to immediately rent out. However, it does take more time. Either way, you need to be able to prequalify to buy the home.

How can you prequalify to buy a home? You could consult with a lender who could provide you a personalized list for exactly what you need to do. Then these items become tasks to complete underneath prequalifying.

Here's an example of the checklist you would develop after unpacking this benchmark:

☐ Obtain rental property that can rent for $5,000 combined per month.
    ☐ Qualify for a home (or my next home) that can rent for at least $1,700 per month.
        ☐ Determine the budget I am comfortable buying within based on rents in the area and running numbers through the risk management formulas.
        ☐ Get with a lender to determine what steps I may need to take in order to qualify, including specific dollar amounts that may be needed.

- ☐ Increase savings to the specific dollar amount the lender provided.
- ☐ Pay off specific dollar amount for debt(s) lender advised.
- ☐ Qualify for a home (or my next home) that can rent for at least $1,700/month
  - ☐ Determine the budget I am comfortable buying within based on rents in the area and running numbers through the risk management formulas.
  - ☐ Get with a lender to determine what steps I may need to take in order to qualify.
  - ☐ Increase savings to specific dollar amount lender provided.
  - ☐ Pay off specific dollar amount for debt(s) lender advised.
- ☐ Qualify for a home (or my next home) that can rent for at least $1,600 per month.
  - ☐ Determine the budget I am comfortable buying within based on rents in the area and running numbers through the risk management formulas.
  - ☐ Get with a lender to determine what steps I may need to take in order to qualify.
  - ☐ Increase savings to specific dollar amount lender provided.
  - ☐ Pay off specific dollar amount for debt(s) lender advised.

When you finish this section of your checklist, you own property that meets the benchmark of rentals that will yield you a combined $5,000 per month. Yes, you will have mortgages, but someone else will be paying those mortgages, and eventually, they will be paid off. You will also have used the tools in your belt for weighing risk, so you will have made good decisions regarding the properties. You do not need to have enough rental property to equal $5,000 per month income; my purpose is to show you how to be specific as you make your checklist.

Follow these same steps for each benchmark you need to reach in order to make it to the future you are envisioning.

If you do not want to handwrite your list, you can use a task management app or software to develop your lists and track your progress. Using software systems that create checklists will help you maximize your time and decrease the time it takes to complete tasks. These types of productivity apps and software are available for free; do not spend money on something fancy to track your checklists.

The tasks are the guideposts you must reach along the way to your goal. It will also keep you on track by enabling you to set timelines and see the big picture.

It is critical not to let yourself become distracted making the checklist to the point where you are paralyzed from starting to complete items on it.

OVERCOME ANALYSIS PARALYSIS

When you are working on a big goal, it is easy to get overwhelmed looking at the big picture. It is better to break that goal down into pieces by identifying benchmarks, then break those benchmarks into tasks that will enable you to reach those benchmarks. Although this process makes approaching the target easier, you can easily get sucked into making the checklist and analyzing each point.

I have seen military members make spreadsheets, then spend hours (spread across days) color coordinating the spreadsheet. Once that's complete, they spend hours (spread across weeks) putting the plan into their calendar and other apps to try to make it all "more efficient." Meanwhile, they lost all that time they could have spent working on the tasks that would enable them to achieve their goals.

To overcome analysis paralysis, prioritize. It will enable you to continue making progress effectively without getting distracted.

If you find yourself getting bogged down by the details (they can easily be overwhelming), look at the list as a whole so that the wrong things don't distract you.

PRIORITIZE

When prioritizing, your goal is to get clear on what needs to be done immediately, what can wait, and what can be delegated to others.

You don't always have to create and tackle checklist tasks in the order you have listed them. Many high-achieving individuals dump everything that needs to be done on a list in no particular order. That way the information is on the paper (or computer) in front of them. They can see everything at once and prioritize it.

When you look at your list, ask yourself these questions:

1. If I don't do this right now, am I negatively impacting someone else?
2. If I don't do this right now, am I negatively impacting myself?
3. What would be the consequences if I didn't do #1 and #2 above? Am I hurting anyone?
4. Do I have what I need to complete this task?

Let's do a nonintimidating example. If the laundry really needs to get washed, ask yourself the following questions:

1. Am I impacting anyone else? The answer is yes—my husband and son.
2. Am I impacting myself? The answer is yes because I won't have clean laundry to wear.
3. What are the consequences if I didn't do the laundry? Am I hurting anyone? The answer is yes because we won't have clean clothes to wear tomorrow.
4. Do I have what I need to complete this task? Yes.

As you move through each item on your checklist, label it with a one, two, or three.

» One stands for: if I don't do this, something bad will happen to me or someone else, or I will let someone down (you also count as "someone").

» Two stands for: this is not a top priority, but it needs to be done, and I need to be the one to do it.

» Three stands for: I can ask someone for help doing this; if no one is available to help, it can wait.

In this laundry example, if I know that I have enough clean clothes for my family to wear tomorrow, washing clothes does not need to be a priority despite the fact that the laundry baskets are full and the clothes need washing. I would label that "two." It is not about procrastinating washing the clothes; it's about recognizing when something else needs to take precedence.

Checklists can be your best friend, but they shouldn't weigh you down. They are a system to move you forward.

CONSISTENCY IS KEY

When looking to accomplish something, especially over the long term, you need to take action consistently.

As you move down your checklist and make progress toward your benchmark, you will activate the part of your brain that loves achievement, which will help keep you motivated to continue. It's crucial to do two things:

1. Consistently look at your checklist.
2. Consistently check off items as you complete them.

If you ever feel unmotivated or that you're not making enough progress, you can easily look back at what you've already accomplished. You can also duplicate and reuse the same checklist (or edit it slightly), which makes the process easier, faster, and less intimidating.

Doing these two simple things will also set you up for taking consistent action toward achieving your goals. If you show up once and it doesn't end up the way you think it should, and you give up trying, how will you ever make big strides toward achieving your goals? For example, say you apply to buy your first house and cannot qualify. Does that mean you will never be able to buy a house? Absolutely not. However, if you never take the necessary actions to move toward that goal, you will not be able to buy a house. This isn't because you couldn't qualify; it is because you didn't do your part—you gave up.

Even if you can qualify, sometimes buying doesn't work out the way you think it should. Many of our clients have a hard time with this; they believe that if they pick their house, make an offer, and negotiate (if necessary), the house will become theirs. And if that doesn't happen because the seller chooses someone else, they take it personally and feel like their entire world is destroyed. Then they give up thinking they will never be able to buy a house. But that only becomes true when you stop consistently trying.

Just because things didn't work out, it doesn't mean that goal is not for you. Explore your options and see where you can go from there.

Consistency wins. Big progress is about making consistent, small actions. Every. Single. Day.

YOU MUST LEAVE THE DRIVEWAY

Don't ever get so caught up in planning your route that you never actually leave the driveway. Don't get so busy looking at all the details, mapping out every mile marker, and determining every site you want to see along the way. If you spend so much time planning the trip and then look back at your life twenty, thirty, forty, or fifty years from now and realize you spent the better part of your time planning instead of starting, experiencing, and enjoying the journey, that's a great tragedy.

Planning where you want to go can be fun and rewarding. You're imagining what your life will look like, and you're putting together a tangible plan that you can easily get excited about. Although it can be intimidating to start that plan, you have to start.

When making checklists, avoid getting so caught up in making the list that you never actually execute on it. Some people create grand checklists they never use.

Pull out of the driveway and start making progress now. Make it a priority so you don't get slowed down and take too long to get to your destination.

QUICK TIPS

» Take the big picture and break it down into smaller pieces. Then ask yourself, "What do I have to do in order to accomplish that piece?" Create your checklist from there. If some items require additional steps, make sure to outline them too. The more unpacked you can get, the more effective you will be.

» When creating your checklist, be detailed in unpacking, but remember, done is better than perfect. Do not let yourself get distracted by things that are not a priority, like making the checklist pretty or not tackling tasks until you feel like the whole list is finished. Planning is great, but execution is what will get you where you need to go.

» Set yourself up for success by committing to taking small action toward your benchmarks every single day. A bunch of small steps compound into big strides and keep you in the marathon.

As you can see, knowing how to check yourself and make sure your anxieties or analysis are not setting you back will enable you to make progress toward your big goals. Unpacking your vision to determine those guideposts, then establishing checklists for reaching them, makes it easier to make progress toward that big goal.

There will always be variables that you cannot see coming or cannot control, but having your checklist will help you focus on what you can control. The goal is not to control everything; the goal is to focus on making what progress you can despite what may come up that tries to pull your attention away from making that progress.

If you allow yourself to become too reactive to what tries to pull away your focus, you will get in your own way. You cannot control the outcome, but you can control your actions and how you react to the scenarios you face. The skill to temper yourself to resist living in constant reactivity is the ultimate freedom.

CHAPTER 9

FREE

RICH ENTERED THE MILITARY AND QUICKLY received his first appointment overseas. While there, he saw all the nasty, ugly things no one dreams of seeing during their lives. Despite what he experienced, Rich served his country, helped his squad, and supported his squadron to make sure they achieved the best possible results.

When he returned home, Rich had amassed significant savings from his deployment pay and wanted to use it for something meaningful. The money signified his time in the military, and it was important to preserve it rather than spend it. Ultimately, he decided to buy a home. To Rich's surprise, he discovered that buying a home with the VA Loan enabled him to purchase his ideal home with very little money out of pocket.

As Rich began the home-buying process, everyone called him crazy. He was a young airman, and he would only be forced to move. But despite their misguided advice, Rich purchased a home.

Over the next few years, Rich focused on learning about real estate and purchasing properties. When he received orders to go to his next duty station, he decided to rent out his current home to a few buddies. He didn't even consider other options because he knew the modest home would make a perfect rental.

At his next duty station, Rich immediately started the home-buying process. Again, everyone told him he was crazy and that it was stupid to buy a home when he knew he would need to move again. But again, Rich stuck to his plan, knowing he was making the right decision based on his future goals.

Several months after moving into his new home, Rich received deployment orders, which would last a minimum of six months. He didn't want to worry about his new home, wanted to ensure the mortgage was paid, and wanted to save his deployment pay, so he obtained roommates to live in the home while he was gone. The mortgage would be paid via the rent the roommates paid, and the house would be taken care of and not abandoned while Rich was gone.

Upon returning from deployment, Rich made the decision to focus on real estate as a means to build his future. He knew that if something went sideways, he could always sell the first home he had purchased because he'd owned it longer and therefore had more equity in it than the second home. Rather than asking the roommates to leave, he continued to rent them the property and began the process of purchasing a third home.

The VA Loan benefit only enables veterans to qualify for specific loan amounts, looking at those amounts in total. Because Rich already owned two properties and was a single-income household, he struggled to qualify for another loan through the VA. That didn't deter Rich. He still wanted to figure out how he could purchase a third property without spending a lot of money out of pocket. Instead of using his deployment money for a down payment on a home, he decided to set his sights on a smaller property and buy a townhome, which costs less than a single-family home.

Yet again, everyone told Rich he was crazy, that he should rent instead of buy. But he knew his plan and that if he stuck to it, owning properties would ultimately provide him with passive income. He moved into the townhome, and about a year later, he received overseas orders that would take him to Korea for twelve to thirteen months.

Knowing that he would be overseas made Rich feel stressed about his investments. Up until this point, he had managed the properties himself. He calculated the benefit of selling the homes versus keeping them and determined that if he kept the properties, they would only increase in value and would provide the needed income he wanted to fulfill his dream of traveling once his military service ended.

Once Rich understood that it was best to keep his properties, he hired a property manager. During his deployment, the bottom fell out of the real estate market. Friends laughed at him and told him he was stupid, questioning why he ever thought it was a good idea to buy the properties, insisting he now had to short sell or foreclose on them because he couldn't afford the mortgage payments.

Rich knew other options must exist. He took a step back, looked at the finances, and realized that as long as he could rent out the properties, he wouldn't have to worry about losing money. Instead of panicking and selling off his properties like so many others did, which he was tempted to do many times, he didn't look at the property values or what he had paid. He only focused on making sure they were rented out, never struggling to find renters because each of his properties was located near military bases with a steady stream of military members coming in and out.

The real estate crash occurred when Rich was about fifteen years through his military career. With prices lower than he'd ever seen them, Rich decided to buy two additional properties, giving him a total of five. He then received overseas orders that would take him to England for a longer period of time. Knowing he could rent out the properties and cover his expenses, Rich chose not to sell. Once the mortgages were paid off, he would own a million-dollar real estate portfolio.

While in England, Rich fell in love with an English woman

and the English countryside. At this time, his investments in the United States were not earning him a lot of money per month, but he had equity in the properties and a great feeling of stability.

Rich completed his twenty years of military service while in England and decided to retire there at the age of forty. He kept his five properties in the United States, and he and his wife invested in real estate in England.

By the time Rich was fifty, his wife owned most of a neighborhood outside of Lakenheath Air Force Base in England. Rich owned ten additional properties in England and five houses in the United States.

At that time, Rich and his wife no longer wanted to work. Traveling the world and having the freedom to do so was their dream, and one they quickly made into a reality.

Slowly, they consolidated their portfolio. Rich sold the first house he had bought, which was almost paid off, and used the equity to pay off two other properties. Then he sold those properties to pay off the remaining two, which he then owned free and clear. As a result of consolidating his portfolio, all rental income now went into Rich's pocket instead of toward paying off mortgages. Not only did Rich gain passive income, but when that income was added to Rich's retirement income from the military, his cash flow equaled more than two times what he had received during active duty.

As you can see, Rich spent his military career focusing on building wealth through real estate wherever he could, which gave him the freedom to enjoy his retirement from the military without having to work.

I'm sure you, too, want financial freedom once you retire from the military, but solely relying on military retirement income is not the best plan. What if you get injured fifteen years into your service? Yes, you'll receive some benefits, but you won't get the same retirement pay that you would have received after twenty years of service. If you don't get injured, your retirement pay will certainly provide income, but will it provide enough income for you to live the life you want?

The choices you make along the way to retirement will determine your success. If you take steps now to set yourself up for retirement, you will gain greater financial freedom.

Fighting for freedom is never a waste. Every single day that you choose to invest, you choose to think outside the box, and you choose to ignore that one supervisor who tries to keep you inside the box by telling you that you're dumb for even considering buying real estate.

The only way to reach out of the box, take control, and have a good shot at freedom is to take steps toward it. You joined the military to fight for our country. Even though you may not be in theater, shooting a gun every day, why wouldn't you take time to fight for your own freedom?

Whether you have served, are serving, or have never come near the military, knowing how to live proactively versus reactively is a key in achieving your goals.

"IT'S THE PRINCIPLE"

People will always be tempted to die on the hill of their opinions; there is no changing that—it is human nature. What is funny is that these opinions vary depending on the person. It's obvious someone would be willing to sacrifice an opportunity if it meant they would lose someone they loved, but every day, you might be sacrificing opportunities because of short-sighted conditioning.

For example, when a buyer goes under contract in Arizona, they have the opportunity to inspect the home and ask the seller to make repairs. These reports are incredibly detailed and note everything from a slightly jiggly front-door handle to a bad roof. The buyer's best strategy is to ask the seller for only the things that really matter. You see, the seller can respond with what they are willing to fix—the longer the list, the less likely they will agree to everything. Plus, if a buyer pads the list with a bunch of small things like loose door handles, but they also want the AC to have its annual maintenance and service prior to moving in, the seller could respond only agreeing to the small, easy fixes rather than the more expensive AC servicing. The AC is working as intended. It's just needing the drain lines blown and routine maintenance, but that would cost more than taking a flathead screwdriver and tightening some doorknobs. The buyer's only option at that point would be to either agree to the seller's repair list or cancel the contract entirely. So, if you aren't strategic in submitting your request, you risk losing the opportunity to buy the home or having to deal with the bigger issues yourself.

I have seen buyers want to cancel a contract for similar reasons. "If they won't do everything we ask, we just won't buy the house," they'd say. That's the limiting principle they chose to stick with. However, because they stuck to that limiting principle, they ultimately lost out on housing security and appreciation just because they felt entitled to a certain response from the seller. That home is worth over $80,000 more now than when they were under contract, while an average AC service in Arizona costs less than $250. They lost out on a potential gain of $79,750 because they chose to stick to a principle—how did that serve their needs?

The inspection report details all items that have been inspected, not just the items that need to be repaired. I've seen sellers lose money because they became emotionally hooked on the inspection report, spending hours of their time picking it apart, feeling offended and questioning the inspector's motives instead of addressing the buyer's actual repair requests. So the sellers end up defensive when responding to items that need to be repaired. But just because something needs to be repaired, it isn't a personal reflection on the seller.

Whether you're a buyer or a seller, it's important to approach the inspection report from a logical investment standpoint rather than an emotional one.

I've seen buyers lose amazing investments because they got so caught up in trying to get the best deal. I've seen sellers scare away good buyers and end up making less with a future buyer than they would have if they had made some repairs for the previous buyer.

See how easily you can become hyperfixated on a specific issue and then lose perspective on the bigger picture? If you don't take in the information and control your reaction to it, you allow yourself to become too reactive and can get in your own way.

Getting emotionally hooked on the idea you had for the outcome, then trying to control that narrative and giving it permission to control how you feel in the moment, resolves nothing. It only makes you frustrated and upset, making it even more difficult to remain objective and make good decisions.

Staying objective and logical is key.

CRABS

If you put a bunch of crabs in a pot, you do need to put a lid on it. Although all the crabs are fully capable of getting out, if one tries, the others pull it back down.

The world today has become very small. Social media has made it possible for people from all sorts of cultures to connect with each other almost instantaneously because information travels at lightning speeds. Yes, there are benefits to this advancement, but the downside is how quickly information can be manipulated and how easily people nowhere near your life can make commentary about how you are living it. It is easier than ever to get pinned down by other people's opinions of you.

If you're more worried about what others think of you than you are about what you think of yourself, then you are shooting yourself in the foot. If you are always focused on what people around you think, you will spend a lot of time and energy trying to show them what you think they want to see instead of making real progress toward the life you want to live. So, if you needlessly spend money on luxuries because you want others to think you are ahead, you are setting yourself back from achieving a long-term goal of financial freedom.

Recognize that you will feel uncomfortable but that if you keep going, you have the best likelihood of reaching your goals. It will be hard when the crabs pulling you down are the people closest to you. This does not mean they do not want you to win—it just means they are scared of what is outside of the pot. Remembering this will help you not take the advice too personally.

For example, if your family tells you it's ridiculous to own multiple homes, look at the positive side of that and think: *They care about me and they're just trying to look out for my best interest. But they don't know what I'm trying to accomplish because they haven't done it themselves. So I'm going to keep moving forward while appreciating that they care enough about me to voice their concerns.*

When you reach for a big goal, people will call you crazy and egotistical. The crabs will claw at you and work to get you back down into the boiling water simply because you are trying to escape it and that scares them. This reaction will challenge any confidence and excitement you may have had when you first started envisioning your goals, which makes it much more difficult to be consistent in making progress and keeping a clear vision of what you want to accomplish.

AVERAGE OF THE FIVE

"You are the average of the five people you spend the most time with."

The late entrepreneur, author, and motivational speaker Jim Rohn said this, and it has been incredibly impactful for me. If your body is what it eats, why wouldn't your mind be what it consumes? When you take a step back and start looking at what you are spending your time watching, listening to, and interacting with, you will likely reveal a lot of limitations you have imposed on yourself.

Becca, Mia, and I were sitting in the office, and I was talking about a book I had read recently: *Untamed* by Glennon Doyle.

Mia got excited hearing about it, so I played the introduction on Audible.

Mia immediately asked to borrow my copy, and Becca looked at me and said, "That's something I never would have known about. Does that actually happen?"

The point isn't the book's subject matter; it's that Becca realized at that very moment how limited her perspective was.

This is what I said to her, which she has mentioned numerous times since it was l life-changing for her to hear:

When you are born, you enter this lane. You are completely unaware of it and spend all of your younger years following it without thinking twice. Who you are around will either widen your existing lane to include more of the same type of people or expose you to the realization that there are other lanes with entirely different beliefs and lifestyles. If you are always around the same kind of people that are like you and your family, you will likely never see that other lanes exist until a moment—like this one you are having now—where it really starts to sink in that you've been in only one lane. It is so easy to just get comfortable in your lane and dig your heels into it, blind to what else is out there, even trying to pull others into your own lane, not realizing the value in an outside perspective. Being challenged, exploring different ways of thinking and what options are out there for you, opens you up to endless opportunities and possibilities. It's a highway, a really big one. You do not have to entirely abandon the lane you came from, but you can change lanes and move around freely to widen your perspective and see what else is out there.

Becca's eyes were wide, and she smiled and even laughed a little. She said, "Wow! I never thought of it that way."

It's your responsibility to change lanes if your existing one is not giving you what you need to thrive. A great way to do this is to absorb content in line with what you are trying to accomplish. You live in a world where inspiring people are more accessible than ever. You can start your day having coffee with Brendon Burchard, get a midday pick-me-up from Tony Robbins, and finish it being soothed to sleep with the intriguing world of Rupi Kaur. Take advantage! Platforms like TikTok, Instagram, YouTube, and others make it easier than ever to access people of incredible wisdom and insight. Take advantage of them too.

QUICK TIPS

» Only you can decide what is most important to you: how you look to others, or if you obtain the life you truly want to live. The sooner you intentionally make this choice, the quicker you will have the freedom to reach your goals.

» Being conscious of who you are surrounding yourself with is a commonly overlooked ingredient to success. It's not all about who you are around in person anymore. With today's technology, you can surround yourself with content in line with your dreams and ambitions, including inspirational people to learn from at no cost other than the device already in your pocket.

» Find someone you may want to emulate, whether that be in the same field or just in the success they have attained; follow them on social media. Learn from them!

In the military, we hear stories where people were able to break from the norm and have great success. Yet we dismiss them because they feel so out of reach. As a result, we don't want to waste our time or money making the attempt.

This is how easy it is to get in your own way. If that's you, recognize this tendency, then look inward to see how you're responding to situations and how you can improve those responses. In doing so, you will also be more resistant to the pressures society places on you as you attempt to do something different by going for your vision.

At the end of the day, the choices you make are yours to make. Write your own story and establish your own freedom. Don't listen to those who question why you are going for something big—those same people have most likely not taken time to decide what they really want and don't understand the benefits in doing so.

Opportunities are available to you if you choose to take them. Use them to obtain the financial freedom to enjoy the life you want.

CHAPTER 10

RIP

MY SON RAN AS FAST AS HE COULD with his little shoes slapping on the wood flooring, giggling as he ran. The house was empty, and he could not resist taking full advantage of the space. I slid down the wall into a seated position on the floor. I was exhausted and relieved he was getting some energy out in a space where I didn't have to worry that he could get hurt.

I had been avoiding his first haircut, knowing how much shorter hair would sharpen his features and make him look older. So his hair floated and flopped around with every step.

We had just closed on this house while my husband had been stationed in Korea for the past eight months. I had done everything for our move: bought a home; lived in a hotel for a bit, waiting for it to close; coordinated military movers; and hauled a chunk of our stuff and vehicles myself, all with the sole purpose of trying to make a life for this little boy that once seemed like a far-fetched dream to me.

As much as I respect military life, those serving our country, and those supporting the ones serving our country, I knew then that I couldn't rely on it to provide what I wanted for my family's future. I wanted freedom for all of us.

I sunk deep into these thoughts as I heard my son's footsteps and laughter echo through the empty home. And as he ran, I visualized what our lives would be and began planning how we would get there.

I decided this home would be the key to unlocking that future. I would learn everything I could about leveraging it in order to become one of those stories that people just don't believe can happen for them, much less in the military. In this moment on the floor, thinking it all through, I had no idea just how far I would be able to take it. But I learned, and then this home with the beautiful sounds of childhood ringing through it became five homes in five years. It became a portfolio that we spent very little out of our pockets to procure.

LEVERAGING REAL ESTATE FOR YOUR FUTURE

The hardest part of investing in real estate is purchasing real estate for the first time. Once you get over your fears, it will open doors for you in the future. You never want to buy a home you can't afford, so ensure the monthly payment makes sense for you.

The beauty of investing in real estate is that it gives you leverage in the future. When we ultimately sold our first home, it was before the tax exemption cutoff for capital gains. We had six figures of equity in the home and were able to divide that equity and purchase two other homes while keeping some of the profit for ourselves.

When investing in real estate, you're slowly building equity, even if there's no appreciation in the marketplace. This is because each month you are applying money toward something you own that can pay you back later versus renting something you will never be able to gain from.

But even if that occurs, your investment will continue to grow. As inflation goes up, the value of the dollar goes down. Therefore, it will take more dollars to purchase your home in the future than it would today. And as the pricing for other goods goes up, the value of your investment will increase as well.

Leveraging real estate enables you to hedge against inflation, unlike stocks and bonds, which are not guaranteed to increase in value. Historically, real estate has realized a steady trajectory in a positive direction at most times. The only time we've seen a decline is when people took out loans for property where the loans were greater than the value of the homes. Lenders did not do their due diligence when writing those loans, enabling people to purchase homes in pet names or without having verified the purchaser's income. That created a bubble that ultimately burst.

Interest rates are a common excuse for not buying a home. Especially in times when they increase. It is so easy for people to get caught up in comparing interest rates and their opinions on how high an interest rate might be. I am honestly not sure if this is a cultural, generational, or military-specific thing, but I constantly hear from my community: "My friend got this interest rate. Why is mine higher?" Each qualification is different, and when the home is being purchased is a factor too. Bust aside from that, what's ironic is that if you are renting a home or living in on-base housing, your interest rate is 100 percent. In other words, your rent is not going toward anything that belongs to you.

Once you make your first real estate investment, you can leverage that investment by giving it a few years to mature and then selling the property, splitting the equity, and using it to purchase two other investments.

Here is the framework I used to leverage the VA Loan along with home equity to own five homes in less than five years:

1. Bought a home with the VA Loan and only paid $3,000 out of pocket to get into this home. Lived in it for two years as a primary residence. We will call this home "A."
2. Got qualified with the VA Loan to buy another home to move into as a primary residence. We will call this home

"B." Only paid $6,000 out of pocket to get into this home. Rented out home "A" when moving into home "B." Lived in home "B" for two years.

3. Sold home "A," which freed up some VA Loan eligibility and gave me more freedom. Now this home had enough cash coming from the sale to be split into two down payments that could later be used to purchase two properties to rent out.

4. Got qualified with the VA Loan to buy another home to move into as a primary residence. We will call this home "C." Home "C" is what we consider our "forever" home, in that we intend to be here until our son graduates high school. I sold home "A" and used money from it to pay the closing costs to get into home "C." Moved from home "B" to home "C" and rented out home "B."

5. Used a conventional loan to buy an investment property to rent out. We will call this home "D." Since I would not be buying a primary residence, I would have to provide a down payment and would have a higher interest rate, but this was okay because I had done my math (see Chapter 6) and the numbers made sense. I used cash from selling home "A" as the down payment.

6. Started shopping for home "E" to use the remaining funds from the sale of home "A" as the down payment for home "E."

We paid $3,000 from savings to buy home "A" and $6,000 from savings to buy home "B." All other costs were covered by the equity cashed in from the later sale of home "A." With the VA Loan, you do not have to provide a down payment as long as you are purchasing within your eligibility. You will still incur closing costs, which are negotiable—the more competitive the market you are in, the more likely you will not be able to negotiate for someone else to pay your closing costs.

I could have refinanced home "A" and pulled cash out of it and then kept it. But in running my numbers (see Chapter 6), it would not have made sense to keep home "A" as a rental property once I pulled cash out, especially considering that I would have exceeded the time frame for the capital gains tax exemption (more details below).

There are many ways to leverage real estate to meet your goals. Let's say my goal was to own home "C" (our "forever" home) outright with no monthly payment. I could have used the same framework to accomplish this goal by making different moves:

1. Buy a home with the VA Loan and only pay $3,000 out of pocket to get into this home. Live in it for two years as a primary residence. We will call this home "A."
2. Get qualified with the VA Loan to buy another home to move into as a primary residence. We will call this home "B." Only pay $6,000 out of pocket to get into this home.

Rent out home "A" when moving into home "B." Live in home "B" for two years.

This is where it gets different…

3. Sell home "A" and set aside all of the cash from the sale to be used as a down payment toward future home "C," even though I do not have to provide a down payment using the VA Loan.
4. Get qualified with the VA Loan to buy another home to move into as a primary residence. We will call this home "C." Move from home "B" to home "C," rent out home "B."
5. Rent out home "B" for roughly three years to let it mature into more equity while someone else (the tenant) is paying the mortgage. Why roughly three years? Because currently the exemption from capital gains taxes with the IRS is that you do not have to pay capital gains tax if you have occupied the home for two of the last five years. So you lived in home "B" for two years, then you need to sell it prior to the five-year anniversary of owning it to avoid throwing a good chunk of change straight to the IRS.
6. Sell home "B" and apply the cash you make from the sale toward the principal balance of home "C."

For us, once we secured home E, the rental income exceeded my husband's income as an active-duty E6 in the Air Force. This was a big benchmark for us to meet.

BUILDING A REAL ESTATE PORTFOLIO

Building a real estate portfolio is customizable based on your goals. We have talked a lot about getting clear on your end goal, visualizing the life you want to live. Building a real estate portfolio is the tool, not the end goal, so do not get it confused. In other words, you can use real estate as a healthy means to achieve the life of your dreams, but just having ten houses for the sake of having ten houses is ego-based, and even if you get them, you will be unsatisfied.

So, figure out what you want the end goal to be then how you can use real estate to get there. Map your route, and set your benchmarks.

For many military members, I recommend a goal centered around making as much money from their investments as they do working in the military. If the home you currently live in could rent out for $2,000 per month and that home's mortgage payment is $1,500, the cash flow on that property would be $500 per month (if it were rented out). Once the mortgage is paid off, the cash flow would be $2,000 (although the actual amount would be higher because as time passes, rents increase by an average of 5 percent annually nationwide, per CoreLogic).

If you want to create $10,000 per month in cash flow from real estate investments, you need to purchase homes whose combined rent equals $10,000. For example, property "A" rents for $2,000 per month, property "B" rents for $1,500 per month, property "C" rents for $2,500 per month, and so on, until they total $10,000. Once those mortgages are paid off, you will have $10,000 in income from those properties. The tenant will be paying the mortgage for you monthly, and you can creatively leverage the properties similar to what I outlined above to pay them off sooner.

EXPENSES

With a mortgage payment comes maintenance and repairs. That's part of owning property. You should set aside money for maintenance, repairs, and other expenses. For example, if you want to hire a property manager[5] instead of taking care of the maintenance yourself, a cost is associated with that. If a property has a homeowners' association (HOA), a cost is associated with that. You can

---

[5]   If you are moving out of state or going overseas, I would recommend hiring a quality property manager. When tenants have difficulty communicating with you, it could open you up to liability and the risk of being sued. A property manager solves that problem. If you live close to your properties and have the time and know-how to make repairs yourself, then do so. Or hire a handyman if you can get one quickly.

factor those expenses into the amount you charge for rent so that you don't bear the burden of those costs.

As rents rise, and they continue to rise over time, expenses tend to remain stable. Yet people often sit across from me and say their reason for not wanting to purchase properties is because if the water heater or air conditioner breaks, they have to buy a new one. If that's what's holding you back, take $500 per month and put it into a savings account and lock it away. Then if you encounter expenses, you can use those savings to pay for them.

When amassing a portfolio, aim to keep your expenses as low as possible. Shorter-term loans can seem favorable because they get paid off more quickly, but that also means eliminating a good chunk of your profit margin from the home rental. You also risk not being able to rent out the home because the cost of the rental must equal or exceed the mortgage payment. And with short-term mortgages, payments are higher than with long-term ones. You don't want to be in a position where, after taking out a short-term loan, you have to sell an investment simply because you can't rent it out for an amount that will cover the mortgage payment.

Taking out a longer-term loan increases the money in your pocket. When you combine that with minimal expenses, you're taking the least amount of risk and giving yourself the highest potential for return.

YOU'RE PLAYING THE LONG GAME

Remember, you're playing the long game. It would be unrealistic to expect to buy five houses in one year and make $10,000 per month on top of your military income. That's not a stable plan. If you set out with that expectation, you will just end up frustrated and give up trying. Stability comes from making smart investments, letting them mature, and not getting scared when one small thing goes wrong.

Do you have to buy real estate to accomplish your goals? No.

Does buying real estate provide the opportunity to significantly propel you toward your goals? Yes.

The options I have shown you are more conservative (safe) than a peer, parent, or onlooker may think; if you rely on their limited perspectives to guide you, it will be really challenging to make big progress. Remember to always think about the experience of the person providing you advice. You will always be criticized by those who have not done what you are attempting to do. Do not make the mistake of taking advice from someone who has not accomplished what you hope to.

The options I've provided you are conservative because you are primarily using the equity earned from the properties to buy more property. You are only coming out of personal savings very little along the way.

If you go to a casino and gamble $100, then you cash out your slip and it says $300, you have won $200 (total cash-out $300 minus initial gamble of $100). The safest thing to do is to put $100 of it back in your pocket and then continue with the $200 in winnings. Real estate is an investment, not a gamble, but what I am teaching you is the same principle. You are reinvesting your winnings (equity earned).

At the moment, I have a few clients whose goals are to buy a home every year. So far, they've been able to do so. The VA does not have a limit on the number of loans you can hold at one time. However, you do have a maximum eligibility. Once you max it out, you have to provide a down payment for additional properties you purchase. If you find yourself in that situation, it's time to weigh other loan types or refinance your first property with a conventional or Federal Housing Administration (FHA) loan, which would give you enough equity for the down payment. Refinancing would prevent you from having to use money out of your pocket for the down payment on the additional property and would enable you to use the equity you've established in the current home instead.

Remember, housing costs will only continue to rise. The more in demand the area is, the more quickly that will occur. Yes, markets operate in cycles and will ebb and flow along the way, but historically the trajectory has been upward. And as generations turn over, housing becomes more strained, so there is no reason why this rise would not continue over time. Even if housing prices don't increase the way you wanted them to (or expected them to), what you owe (the amount still owed on your mortgage) will slowly decrease, and you can ultimately rent that property and generate passive income.

QUICK TIPS

» If you don't already own real estate property, start looking at the steps you need to take to start investing, including your eligibility for the VA Loan.

» If you have a first investment, make sure you leverage it mindfully. How you leverage your first investment sets the tone for future investment, so it's best to use a professional to help you do so.

» Find me on social media—Instagram and TikTok @calzajulie, calzaco on Facebook—and follow so I can coach you through your process with free tips and guidance. You can leave your questions as comments there, and I will answer them personally.

There's a saying that the best time to plant a tree was twenty years ago, but the second-best time is now. Whether you're in your twenties and have just arrived at your first duty station, you're retiring from the military, or you're somewhere in between, make investing in real estate a priority so you don't get slowed down and take too long to get to your destination. The sooner you start, the more opportunities you have along the way.

What matters most to me is that you have a choice. In the future, you don't want to be someone who, after having served your country, is forced to take a job you don't want in order to provide for yourself and your family. Investing in real estate will give you freedom of choice because you'll have more stability, more income, and more access to money than if you didn't take this route.

CHAPTER 11

EXTRA

WHEN I WAS YOUNG MY DAD REALLY PUSHED me to become a strong swimmer. Some of my earliest memories (at two to three years old) were when he would take me to the lake or public pool and throw my figurines in the water and have me dive to retrieve them.

Then when I was about six years old, it was kind of like I graduated. We would go to the river where tourists would ride inner tubes, drinking and having fun. There were some rapids along the way, nothing one in a tube couldn't navigate—if they fell out, most of them could stand or quickly get to an area where they could.

But the rapids were strong enough to cause the tourists to flip over often. My dad spent so much time there that he could predict who might flip as they were floating down the river. He coached me how to do the same. We frequented these spots where they would flip, and my dad taught me to "dive for treasure."

He would have me "geared up" in a bathing suit, old tennis shoes, a tattered fanny pack around my waist, a mask, and a snorkel. Then he would assign me an area, while he worked another area further away. It was my job to find the things tourists dropped and put any "treasure" I found in my fanny pack under the water, unseen. I got the most praise if I found the baggies of cash people would frequently bring with them on their floats, or wallets with cash in them. For the wallets, my dad would take out the cash as a "finder's fee" then mail the wallet and the rest of its contents to the address on the ID or turn it in to the closest local business's lost and found. It was not uncommon to find jewelry or even clothing. If we found clothing and it was our sizes, we kept it; if not, we threw it onto the shore.

My dad would sell the sunglasses (Oakleys, Ray-Bans, and Maui Jims were the best to get) and jewelry out of the trunk of the car.

Police would walk the banks of the areas we "worked" during holiday weekends, but as the years went by, they were out more and more. I could tell there was tension and was taught to fear the police and to always stay in the water since it was a public waterway.

All tourist season, this is what we did, and this is how my dad made money.

I was taught that the world was against us and that there was always someone or something out to take from us. The environment I grew up in made it seem like I would have to work incredibly hard just to make ends meet, and I'd be lucky to score a job making $30,000 working as someone's assistant—that should be the goal, it seemed. My mom worked so hard, mostly as a single mom, when I was growing up. She did the best she knew how and taught me to be grateful for anything I got and not to expect more. She didn't want me to be disappointed. My dad taught me to hustle and not be afraid, to be tough. While I may now disagree with their tactics as a parent myself, I appreciate how these lessons molded me into someone unwilling to settle and unwilling to trade my integrity for anything. More than anything, I wanted to prove I could do more, that I could be the person able to afford the vacation to the cool river with my loving family anytime I wanted. Not the person having to dive for missing treasures to sell out of the trunk of a beat-up car.

I set a goal to make six figures in one year by the time I retired. I had heard that people could make money like that, and I had seen on TV that they mostly wore suits and worked at big companies. So I decided that's what I would do. It felt like such an audacious goal but one I was determined to accomplish, although I thought I would have to work for twenty years and climb a corporate ladder to do so. I was more than willing to do the work. At seventeen I realized I really needed a way out of the small town my mom and I were living in. I had great grades in school, but I decided

I needed to go a different route, something other than trying to make ends meet working through college on scholarship, so I asked my mom to sign off on emancipation so I could join the Marine Corps. Then I went to work.

The first time I bought a home, the concept of making money by buying homes felt like a scam. It did not feel real that I would ever make more than I paid for the house if I sold it later. I was just buying it because I was young and dreamed of owning a home and was able to qualify. It cost me next to nothing out of pocket to buy it. Down the road, when I sold that home, I made six figures. It still didn't feel right, like I had done something illegal and that someone would come and take the money from me. When neither of these things happened, I realized not enough people in my lane—in my community—knew about this type of opportunity. I wanted to teach them; honestly, I wanted to save them like I had been trying to save myself.

It is not about the six figures at all. It's about how investing in real estate can provide for a future you thought you'd have to work twenty years to come close to achieving.

OVERCOMING TOXICITY

Whenever we face something challenging, our survival instincts make us want to alleviate the discomfort as quickly as possible, to do whatever it takes to return to what feels safe. But growth does not happen without discomfort. When you go to the gym and lift weights to grow muscles, you feel sore afterward because you rip those muscles in order to grow new fibers.

You feel incredibly uncomfortable when working to accomplish difficult goals, especially big financial goals, and especially if you grew up in an environment where accomplishing those goals seemed impossible.

Those crabs are everywhere. If you have a goal to retire at age forty, and those around you tell you you're supposed to work until sixty-five or seventy, the toxicity of those opinions limits your ideas and your potential. To avoid the toxicity, have the confidence to know that what you are trying to accomplish is possible, no matter how impossible it may seem.

Recognize that you will feel uncomfortable, but if you keep going, you have the best likelihood of reaching your goals.

Your goal is attainable. But if you don't even try, you miss 100 percent of the shots you didn't take. And you'll never reach your goal.

When you're ready to reach toward financial freedom, the best way to do so is by conscientiously moving forward and making slow progress toward that goal. If you try to go too fast too soon, you'll burn out.

DON'T BE IN A HURRY

Stepping into the arena, getting messy, taking action, and doing things spectators around you might be discouraging you from doing is not easy work. There are a ton of "overnight" success stories out there, but it takes years of consistent action and progress for that overnight success to occur.

When people refer to my mentor, Lizy, their perception is that she was an overnight success. Yes, she is hugely successful and top-ranked nationwide in her field, but it took her eight years of working on her business, of engaging in consistent action over time, to become an "overnight success."

I sit across from families eager and ready to sell investments because they want to walk away with money from the sale. They had never imagined they could ever have so much money, so when they see it, they want to cut and run, even if they don't have a plan of what they're going to do next.

I coach and reassure the families on how to leverage that money to make even more, despite their fears that they must take the money now or they might never get it—and especially when they're dreaming of buying a boat or a car.

I'm not saying you shouldn't sell. But when you do, take care to leverage the money in a way that will ensure you make more money from it. Doing so will give you financial freedom once you leave military life.

Most people, whether they're in the military or not, aspire to obtain financial freedom that gives them the opportunity to work when they choose or take a job they really love because they don't have to be stressed over income. Some people have the courage to reach for it; others do not.

APPRECIATE THOSE WITH YOU
ON THE JOURNEY

As you set goals, it's important to appreciate those in your life who are supporting you (spouse, kids, significant other, even yourself). When you don't try, you not only take away opportunities from yourself but from them too. You also inhibit others from trying or thinking they can be successful. When you reach for your goals, you influence others even when you don't realize you are doing so. It's your duty to try and to influence others in moving toward financial success postmilitary.

QUICK TIPS

>> If you don't step into the arena, you automatically fail. If you put one foot in front of the other, no matter how small the steps might be, you make small progress toward bigger goals.

>> Concern yourself with your own perspective rather than listening to what others say. Go for your goals and don't be concerned with who might be watching. They may see something as a miss when it's really the next thing that is propelling you toward a dream you may still doubt is even possible.

>> Remember, this is not an instant process. You won't get your Amazon instant gratification here. This is the long game, but it is worth it because it is your life.

No one makes 100 percent of their shots. You may only see the wins and not the mountain of misses behind them.

What's the worst that could happen if you try?

Maybe you do not perfectly end up where you thought you wanted to go, but what if you end up somewhere even better?

CONCLUSION

THE MAXIMUM AMOUNT OF TIME you can serve in the military leaves you with a whole lifetime postmilitary. I know you don't want to get out of the military after twenty years and be forced to work at a job you don't like just to make ends meet. I know you want financial freedom for your postmilitary life. The only way to ensure that occurs is to enter the arena and take steps now to secure that future.

Understand your goals and reach for them, or you will never benefit. If you don't try, you risk living your life in a middle-ground loop, never escaping paycheck-to-paycheck living. It may not feel "bad" per se, but you are not moving toward anything; you're just stagnant, standing still with no progress toward a real goal like financial independence.

Yes, you can take your time to make progress, but life passes quickly, so do not put it off. Start taking the necessary steps to achieve what you really want.

Stretch outside the box that we are put into as military members and military families. As you do so, you will inspire others to do the same. That's where change really occurs. That's where we see the rate of homeless veterans go down. That's where we see the rates of people seeking help for PTSD go up, which decreases the rate of veteran suicide.

These changes happen from within. It's up to us.

When you step into the arena, you're not just doing it for yourself; you're doing it for everyone watching you. They can see you take risks and courageously continue to try to achieve your goals when they might not think it's even worth trying.

Putting one foot in front of the other and taking small steps forward shows others they shouldn't be afraid to try, to challenge what they've been told, and to think differently.

Feel proud that you step into the arena. If you're successful, you get to live a life you thought was only for others. Take pride in that accomplishment. And if you're not successful, you get to take your last breath knowing you tried, rather than never taking a step and wondering what could have happened if you had tried.

We all cross the finish line of life one day. Take the shots.

Even if there's only a 1 percent chance that you might be successful in whatever you are attempting to achieve, why not try? You could be that one person out of a hundred who is successful. But I'm here to tell you: your odds are substantially better than that and well within your control.

I wrote this book for you, the people who have so much noise around you, who have to try to thrive in an environment you have no control over. My goal is to show you the areas where you can take back control and to empower you to break through the noise.

This book is also for you, the people who are trying to navigate this life and support your loved ones through it. Life tries to put us in boxes. But while you're in the box, you might as well paint that sucker up, make it pretty, and prepare so that you can maximize the moment when the tape loosens.

This is your real life.

And this is your real battle cry.

Take steps now to build your postmilitary life. Get up, get out there, and start putting one foot in front of the other.

I've got your back.

Be sure to visit www.postmilitaryfuture.com for book resources, additional information, and exclusive content that did not make it into the book. There you can also join my free monthly email newsletter, complete with breaking advice, a reading list, and more interactive content.

If you need hands-on help, be sure to follow me on social media. It's free and I post daily on most platforms and answer all comment questions. You can also message me directly. Find me on Instagram and TikTok @calzajulie, calzaco on Facebook, or on YouTube by searching Julie Calza.

ACKNOWLEDGMENTS

THIS ENTIRE PROJECT would not have come to fruition without the unyielding support of my amazing husband. Cedrick, you are the love of my life. I am grateful for every day I get with you.

Liam Calza, I am so incredibly proud of you. You are so kind and talented. I love you forever, no matter what, and will continue to support you wherever you go.

Strider, forgive me for ignoring the thirty-three thousand balls you must've dropped in my lap or at my feet along the way.

Mom, thank you for your courage—it really is all good, I promise.

Lizy Hoeffer, thank you for pushing me when I needed it and encouraging me to rest when I didn't think I deserved it (whether I listened or not, I appreciate it).

The CalzaCo crew, you are the people I can trust to care about our community and respect what we do. My team represents those who trust us with the same level of dedication I founded this business on. They love my people—our people—and help me to pour everything we can into supporting military members and their families in taking control of what they can. They adapt and overcome with our clients; they stay ahead of an incredibly challenging industry. They innovate alongside me. They believe in our mission, and they make it possible for CalzaCo to be a safe place for our clients to reach their real estate goals so they can more quickly reach their financial ones. Thank you all from the absolute bottom of my heart for supporting me through this. Niki, I feel like I never would have finished without you.

My community, I do not think I have words to adequately convey my gratitude for all of you who have trusted CalzaCo to provide you services and give you guidance, but I will try. I was terrified when I started this business. I did not want to be a business owner; I did not want to be responsible for leading all on my own. I saw a need and I couldn't find an available solution. Every company I looked into wasn't prioritizing the people I wanted to help. Since I couldn't find the solution, I resolved that I would become it.

From the beginning, the support I received from the local community was beautiful, and it made me want to work harder for you every day. You believed in me when I wasn't sure if I was good enough. You left me reviews that shone like sunlight through storm clouds on my hardest days, and you told your friends and everyone you worked with about my services. As I grew, you helped me welcome new members and trusted my judgment. The CalzaCo proven process, our amazing statistics, and this very book are all a result of your support. I deeply appreciate everyone who has been a part of my story, and I remain incredibly grateful for your continued support of my business.

I sincerely thank my media and publishing team. Your loyalty to what I wanted to convey and putting up with my stubborn opinions made this book come together better than I imagined. Janice, you pulled out of me some of what I didn't want to give. I appreciate your patience and thank you for not sugarcoating it along the way.

Thank you, reader, for reading or listening to this book. It is a lot to take in. My hope is that you found something that will help you make incredible progress toward living the life of your dreams. That thing might just be reminding yourself to imagine it and to envision what it will be like to live in that dream regularly. Simply by taking the time to read something that could help, you have already made progress in shaping it into reality.

CPSIA information can be obtained
at www.ICGtesting.com
Printed in the USA
BVHW041942120223
658271BV00033B/714/J

9 781544 531632